America's

BLACK

COLLEGES

J. WILSON BOWMAN, Ph.D.

DISCARD

$14.95

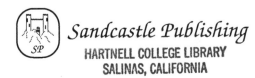
Sandcastle Publishing
HARTNELL COLLEGE LIBRARY
SALINAS, CALIFORNIA

AMERICA'S BLACK COLLEGES
The Comprehensive Guide to Historically & Predominantly Black 4-Year Colleges & Universities

Copyright © 1992 by J. Wilson Bowman
Book Interior & Cover Design by R. Rolle-Whatley

This publication is designed to provide accurate and authoritative information in regard to the subject covered. Although the author has exhaustively researched all sources to ensure the accuracy and completeness of the information contained in this book, both author and publisher assume no responsibility for errors, inaccuracies, omissions or any other inconsistency herein. Any slights against people or organizations are unintentional. Readers should contact the schools of their choice for complete up-to-date information on tuition fees, expenses and courses offered.

Publisher's Cataloging in Publication
(Prepared by Quality Books Inc.)

Bowman, J. Wilson
America's black colleges : the comprehensive guide to historically & predominantly black 4-year colleges & universities / J. Wilson Bowman ; foreword by Marva N. Collins.
p. cm.
Includes bibliographical references and index.
ISBN 0-9627756-1-4

1. Afro-American universities and colleges--Guide-book. 2. Afro-American universities and colleges--History--Guide-books. I. Title. 3. Universities and colleges--United States. 4. Church schools--United States--History.

| LC2781.B6 1992 | 378.73 | 92-60007 |

Printed in the United States of America

6 5 4 3

Dedication

**To African-American Youth
who must realize that
in their struggle for truth,
education is the only road to freedom**

Acknowledgements

This book is intended primarily to assist the many high school students and their parents, counselors, and college administrators who are in search of an affordable and rewarding institution of higher learning.

My sincere thanks and appreciation . . .

To Dr. Joan Clinton who read every page,

To all of those who said "That's a good idea" and those who helped bring this reference guide to fruition,

To the staff at the colleges and universities who responded to my letters and calls for information,

To those who believed in the value of the book,

To Sandcastle Publishing for unflagging faith in the book and especially to Renee, my editor, who coordinated the project in addition to designing the book's interior and its cover. Working with Sandcastle Publishing has indeed been a pleasure,

And most of all to Richard—the wind beneath my wings.

Contents

Contents

Foreword

The Age of Reason, the Age of Analysis, and the Age of Ideology represent the history of civilization. We as a people must return to the Age of Analysis. Dr. King followed the examples of Martin Buber, Thoreau, Emerson, Aristophanes, Euripides and Gandhi. It is time that students begin to study the thought of these great men; add some of their own thought, and do something with their lives. Our dilemmas are not exclusively Black ones, they are dilemmas shared by mankind. We must realize that strides made by any people have not been easy.

This must become the Age of Black College Survival. Without Black colleges, Blacks never could have made the financial and economic strides evident today. However, our people are nevertheless floating on a rising tide of mediocrity, complacency and handwringing, lamenting the difficulties of making it against such Herculean odds. We must summon the Black colleges to help us succeed. Our freedom has been bought with sweat, blood, tears, determination, curiosity, forebearance and hard work. The role of the Black college is to teach our children how to acknowledge our merits, cultivate them and succeed.

Our Black colleges have dared to accept impossible challenges—and they have found glorious things in our young. How many of our students learn for themselves, for their own betterment, rather than having assignments merely thrust upon them? Readers are leaders. Thinkers succeed. Determination and perseverance move the world; thinking that others will do it for us is a sure way to fail. Only Black colleges can say this to students without risk of being misunderstood.

Who will teach our children to read *The New York Times* bestseller list each week, to know what is going on in the world besides the latest top ten record listing; to dare to dream; to dare to aspire? Only Black colleges can dare our students to dream not only of buying that dream house with the two-car garage, but also of owning the car franchise itself.

Black colleges in the past became mentors, surrogate parents and beacons imparting light to the hopeless. Today, these colleges with the same deliberation have dared use their faculties and commitment to bring to useful fruition minds that might otherwise have been wasted. Black colleges make the impossible possible.

Most Black colleges accept our students when other institutions would not accept them, with their abysmal test scores and poor preparation. This means that these students have an obligation to work twice as hard to master those skills that they have not already been taught. They must prove that they can become scholars and contributors to the world.

It has been through my determination to succeed, that I have been able to bring pride to my people, to my college (Clark College in Atlanta) and to my family. I sought to be superior in whatever I did—not for me, but for those who must follow. I doubt if I could have felt so strongly the needs of my people without a Black college experience. I removed myself from the "Age of the Shrug" with its "so-what-it-is-not-my-problem" attitude, because this is what I was taught in a Black college.

Much has been taken from us as a people. With Black colleges much still abides. They are promoters of excellence, self-esteem, pride in race, and hope for the future. With tempered hopes and determined faith, we will emerge as a new order in society. We must maintain our legacy in Black colleges—the only chance for some, a second chance for others. *We, too, are achievers. We, too, can become excellent.* Let us pull together to maintain the vibrancy and viability of Black colleges.

— *Marva N. Collins*

Founder, Director Westside Preparatory School
Chicago, Illinois
December 12, 1991

Introduction

Between the end of the Civil War and the beginning of World War I, several educational foundations were established specifically to advance the education of Blacks in America. The Peabody Education Fund, the General Education Board, the Anna T. Jeanes Fund, the Julius Rosenwald Fund, and the Caroline Phelps-Stokes Fund were among the philanthropists that contributed substantially toward bringing about a new day for education in the South. By the 1900s, there were 28,560 schools focused on the preparation of teachers for Black Schools throughout the South.

Today, there are 100 historically and/or predominantly Black four-year colleges and universities. For most of these their names are not household words. But their mission is sharply focused, offering some of the best bargains in higher education in the United States. Most of these small, scholarly enclaves devote themselves to undergraduates. The student/faculty ratio is usually low, averaging fifteen-to-one. The schools are not as selective as the larger more expensive schools. They are less likely to screen out promising minority students.

Several factors have given **Historically and/or Predominantly Black Colleges and Universities (H/PBCUs)** appeal. Among these are: small class size, reasonable tuition, close student/professor relationships, supervised living environments and challenging opportunities rarely afforded Black students in majority institutions. These campuses provide role models and mentors, and there is no subtle discouragement, no lowered expectation.

The H/PBCUs offerings are from Aerospace to Fashion to Veterinary Medicine. The curriculum for most of the four-year institutions has a common core - a foundation of general education. This foundation usually covers the first two years of the four-year degree curriculum. It consists of courses from each of the following broad subject matter areas - English, mathematics, social and behavioral science, history, natural science, and humanities - with units ranging from 20 to 32 semester hours. The minimum credit-hour load for a full-time undergraduate student working towards the bachelor's degree is 12 hours per semester. A normal load for a full-time undergraduate student in good standing is 15 to 18 semester hours.

The primary responsibility of the H/PCBU is to provide academic programs which allow each student to acquire and develop skills which are necessary in today's competitive society.

Admission is based upon receipt of an official application, a copy of all transcripts, a medical examination together with a health history questionnaire and a high school diploma (or GED) illustrating completion of the following:

- 4 years of English
- 2 years of Mathematics
- 2 years of Natural Science
- 2 years of Social Science

The SAT or ACT scores may or may not be required, but it is highly recommended.

Transfer students can transfer a maximum of 70 units (credit hours) but must have a "C" (2.0) average on a 4-point scale in the following 24 semester hours: English Composition-6 units; College Algebra-3 units; Laboratory Science-6 units; Electives-9 units.

In order to receive the baccalaureate degree, most of the institutions require students to maintain a grade-point average of 2.0, spend a minimum of two terms in residence, and complete an exit competency examination in writing and mathematics.

Housing opportunities vary from campus to campus. Those that provide on-campus residence usually accommodate a limited number of students. Priority is generally based upon the date of application, i.e. first-come first-served.

Most of the H/PBCUs provide an array of student organizations open to all students who qualify. This would include Greek fraternal organizations such as Alpha Phi Alpha, Omega Psi Phi, Kappa Alpha Psi, Phi Beta Sigma, and sororities such as Alpha Kappa Alpha, Sigma Gamma Rho, Delta Sigma Theta, and Zeta Phi Beta.

Honor societies such as the following are found on many of the H/PBCUs' campuses: Alpha Chi, Alpha Kappa Mu, Alpha Phi Sigma, Beta Kappa Chi, Kappa Delta Phi, Phi Beta Lambda, Phi Alpha Theta and Sigma Rho Sigma.

In addition to the national organizations, professional societies and honor societies, opportunities to participate in student government, student newspaper, the yearbook, dramatics, recitals, concerts, art activities and athletic events are also available on the campuses. These organizations afford students the opportunity to develop leadership skills and teamwork abilities - benefits that would be rare at major universities.

History has shown that African-Americans attending H//PCBUs are more likely to complete a degree than those attending predominantly non-minority institutions. In 1984-85, HBCUs awarded 34% of the baccalaureate degrees earned by Blacks, while enrolling only 18% of the Black college students. This diverse group of institutions has provided the passage to middle-class for countless Blacks from poverty-ridden areas of the rural south and inner-cities.

Black colleges shape the future of Black America. These institutions were designed to meet the unique educational and social needs of the African-American. Most colleges are small and truly struggling; - they are doing much with little. While the H/PBCUs offer the usual general education courses they have much more to offer. The level of opportunity and self-respect that decades of integration have not been able to duplicate is the hall-mark of the Black institutions. The fact that these institutions can still relate to students from rural areas and poor socio-economic backgrounds and place them in mainstream American society is in itself a colossal accomplishment.

The H/PBCUs are institutions that are committed. They provide a special environment at an important time in the life of the young adult. They give the African-American youth a sense that they are in charge and that success is attainable.

A year at schools like Pepperdine and USC can cost as much as $20,000, whereas the H/PBCUs provide a high quality education at a much reduced price. The average cost for tuition, fees, room and board at a private four-year institution is around $12,000. The average cost at the H/PBCUs is about $6,000. Additional costs will vary depending upon the student's life-style, the location of the college (urban/rural), and academic major selected.

There is no doubt that the historically and/or predominantly Black colleges and universities offer a great deal that should be seriously considered when planning for an education beyond high school.

—J. Wilson Bowman
Tuskegee University Alumni

Financial Aid For Education

Education after high school costs more than ever before. It is vital that students planning to enter college learn about as many sources of aid as possible. Some suggestions follow:

(1) Contact the financial aid administrator at each school that you would like to attend, and ask for information about the aid programs available and the current total cost of education at the college.

(2) Ask your state higher education agency for information about state aid. Each state has its own programs with award levels, eligibility criteria, and application procedures. For information, call 1-800-4 FED AID.

(3) Check foundations, religious organizations, fraternities, sororities, and town and city clubs for scholarship information. Include community organizations such as Soroptomist, Jaycees, Chamber of Commerce, etc. Also . . .

> • Many companies and labor unions have programs to help pay the cost of college education for family members of employees.

> • Academic scholarships are available from the National Merit Scholarship and National Honor Society.

(4) Throw an "Off to School-Scholarship Shower", similar to bridal and/or baby showers, and invite all of those individuals who would want to see you become a college student.

In today's market, it is necessary that you participate in the funding of your education. A college education costs time, money and effort. To ensure getting into the school of your choice, do not wait until you finish high school.

In your junior year—
- Take college preparatory classes.
- Check with your counselor about taking the preliminary scholastic aptitude test (PSAT), attend college fairs, collect brochures.
- Take the PSAT in preparation for the SAT.
- Take the SAT.

In your senior year—
- Select at least three colleges, obtain brochures and applications.
- Meet with your counselor for assistance in completing one of the applications.
- Contact teachers who will prepare letters of recommendation.
- Complete and mail applications.
- Repeat the SAT if necessary.
- Complete and submit student aid applications with the assistance of a financial aid specialist.

Results of admissions and financial aid arrive before June.

The cost of a college education increases yearly. To obtain current fees information for the college of your choice, contact the school directly. (See Appendix A for the address.)

Facts About H/PBCU Graduates

✔ Over eighty-five percent of African-American veterinarians in the United States graduate from Tuskegee University.

✔ Nearly half of the African-American health-care professionals in Mississippi are Tougaloo graduates.

✔ A greater percentage of Fisk graduates achieve the Ph.D. degree than the minority graduates of any other U.S. college or university.

✔ Approximately three percent of the African-American lawyers are alumni of Morehouse.

✔ Eighteen college presidents are graduates of Virginia Union University.

✔ Twenty percent of the public school teachers and administrators in New Orleans are graduates of Dillard University.

✔ Grambling College has placed more football players in the professional ranks than any other college.

The Ten Largest H/PBCUs

University	Enrollment	Percent Black
Howard University	12,500	80
University of D.C.	11,000	80
Southern University (BR)	9,200	92
Tennessee State	8,000	63
Texas Southern	7,500	73
Norfolk State	7,400	87
Florida A&M	7,200	84
Grambling	7,000	97
Jackson State	6,500	93
North Carolina A&T	6,200	82

Alabama

8 H/PBCUs

ALABAMA AGRICULTURAL AND MECHANICAL UNIVERSITY

Alabama A & M University started in 1875 as a junior college with two teachers and sixty-five students. William Hopper Council, an ex-slave, served as president of the college for approximately thirty-five years. The school was organized as a state normal school and became a land-grant college in 1891.

Joseph Fanning Drake took over the presidency in 1922 and the institution developed from a junior college to a four-year college offering degrees from five undergraduate schools and a school of graduate studies. From a 200-acre plot purchased in 1891, the site has expanded to encompass more than 2000 acres.

CHRONOLOGY OF NAME CHANGES

1875	-	Huntsville Normal School
1878	-	State Normal and Industrial School
1919	-	The State Agricultural and Mechanical Institute for Negroes
1948	-	Alabama Agricultural and Mechanical College
1969	-	Alabama Agricultural and Mechanical University

LOCATION

The picturesque hillside campus is composed of handsome red-brick buildings, sweeping lawns, wooded areas, drives and walkways. In addition there are more than 30 major buildings including an athletic complex, a Fine Arts center, a student center, 20 institutional facilities, 11 dormitories, the cafeteria and a learning resource center/library.

The college is located in Huntsville, a city with a population of approximately 170,000. Birmingham is the nearest metropolitan area.

The Address: **Alabama A & M University**
                    Huntsville, Alabama 35762
                    Telephone: (205) 859-7011

THE INSTITUTION

A & M is a medium size historically Black, co-educational, state-supported institution and land-grant college which awards the Baccalaureate and Master's degrees. It has an enrollment of approximately 4200 students and a student/faculty ratio of fourteen-to-one.

There are five undergraduate schools -

- The School of Agriculture and Home Economics
- The School of Arts and Science
- The School of Business
- The School of Education
- The School of Technology

The School of Graduate Studies grants degrees in sixty-three areas.

Dual-degree, reciprocal, and/or cooperative programs are available in various fields with the following institutions:

Athens State College
Georgia Institute of Technology
John C. Calhoun State Community College
Oakwood College
Tuskegee University
University of Alabama
University of Tennessee

FEES

Cost per academic year: Tuition $2400, room and board $2000.

DISTINGUISHED ALUMNI

James Turner	-	Political leader
Dr. Patricia Elzie	-	Professor of Education Albany State College
Philip Jackson	-	1982 Golf Director Dept. of Parks & Recreation Los Angeles
Dr. Herman E. Walston	-	Professor of Home Economics Kentucky State University
Dr. Earl Roberson Sr.	-	President Carver Technical College, AL

ALABAMA STATE UNIVERSITY

After beginning as a private school in 1866 for the education of Blacks, the school was chartered as a public institution in 1874. Originally located in Marion, Alabama, the school moved to Montgomery in 1887. The institution became a four-year institution in 1929. The first Baccalaureate degree was awarded in 1831.

CHRONOLOGY OF NAME CHANGES

1874	-	State Normal School and University for Colored Students and Teachers
1887	-	Alabama Colored Peoples University
1889	-	State Normal School for Negroes
1946	-	Alabama State College for Negroes
1954	-	Alabama State College
1969	-	Alabama State University

LOCATION

The university is an urban campus in the capital of Alabama. There are numerous shopping areas and good restaurants. Churches of various denominations are within walking distance of the University. The city has an excellent bus system, and air travel and passenger rail service is readily available.

The Address: **Alabama State University
915 South Jackson Street
Montgomery, Alabama 36195
Telephone: (205) 293-4100**

THE INSTITUTION

Alabama State is a co-educational institution. With an average enrollment of 4000 students, it has a student/faculty ratio of twenty-to-one. Students from Alabama share the friendly campus atmosphere with students from twenty-four other states and six foreign countries.

Student life at the University offers opportunities for students to participate in student government, a student newspaper, the yearbook, dramatics, forensics, musical recitals and art activities. There are four chapters of national fraternities and four of national sororities as well as nationally chartered professional societies and honor societies.

The University is divided into four degree granting divisions:
- The College of Arts and Science
- The College of Business Administration
- The College of Education
- The College of Music

The baccalaureate degree is granted in the following areas: accounting, art/art-education, biology, business administration/ education, chemistry, computer science, criminal justice, drama, economics, education, English, finance, French, health and physical education, history, human services, journalism, laboratory technology, marine science, mathematics, music, mass communication, physics, political science, psychology, sociology, Spanish and speech.

FEES

Cost per academic year: tuition, room and board $6000 to $7000.

DISTINGUISHED ALUMNI

Yvonne Kennedy, Ph.D. - President, Bishop Junior College, 1991-92 National President of the Delta Sigma Theta sorority

Bishop Joseph L. Howze - Bishop of Biloxi, MS Catholic Archdiocese

MILES COLLEGE

Miles College was founded in 1905 by the Christian Methodist Episcopal Church. It is private and co-educational. For the first half of the twentieth century, Miles College was the only four-year college in metropolitan Birmingham open to Black students. The first postsecondary level offering was in 1907 and the first baccalaureate degree was awarded in 1911.

CHRONOLOGY OF NAME CHANGES

    1905 -   Miles Memorial College
    1911 -   Miles College

LOCATION

The college is located in the western section of Birmingham on thirty-five acres with twenty-one buildings. Transportation to and from the campus is available on the public bus transit system. Most of the major airlines service the Birmingham area. Passenger rail service is also available.

The Address: **Miles College**
                      5500 Myron Massey Blvd.
                      Birmingham, Alabama 35208
                      Telephone: (205) 923-2771

THE INSTITUTION

Miles College is a small college with an average enrollment of 500 students. On-campus housing is provided for approximately 50 percent of the student body. The student faculty ratio is about twelve-to-one.

The bachelor's degree is offered in the following areas: biology, business administration, chemistry, communication, education, English, language arts, mathematics, music, political science and social science.

Pre-professional programs are available in Dentistry and Medicine at the college; as well as cooperative programs in engineering and veterinary medicine with Tuskegee University. Other dual-degree programs are offered with the University of Alabama in nursing and the allied health occupations.

FEES

Cost per academic year: tuition, room and board $6000.

DISTINGUISHED ALUMNI

Dr. Perry W. Ward   -   President, Lawson State
                                 Community College
Andrew Sneed Jr.   -   Special Program Coordinator
                                 Alabama State University

OAKWOOD COLLEGE

Oakwood College was established by the Seventh-Day Adventist Church on a one-thousand-one-hundred-and-eighty-five-acre site in Huntsville, Alabama in 1896. It is a private college affiliated with the General Conference of Seventh-day-Adventist.

CHRONOLOGY OF NAME CHANGES

1896	-	Oakwood Industrial School
1904	-	Oakwood Manual Training School
1917	-	Oakwood Junior College
1944	-	Oakwood College

LOCATION

The college is located in the north-central part of the state approximately 100 miles from Birmingham to the south and Chattanooga, Tennessee on the east. It is a relatively small, friendly town with an airport within ten miles of the campus.

The Address: **Oakwood College**
Oakwood Road
Huntsville, Alabama 35896
Telephone: (205) 726-7030

THE INSTITUTION

The average enrollment at the college is approximately 1200. On-campus residence halls house seventy-seven percent of the student body and the student/faculty ratio is approximately twenty-to-one. The curriculum is varied offering dual-degree programs and cross-registration with several schools: dual-degree in architecture and engineering at Tuskegee University and cross-registration with

Alabama A and M University, Athens State College, and the University of Alabama. A veterinary medicine program is available through the Consortium.

The associate and bachelor's degrees are award in the following: accounting, agricultural science, allied health fields, biochemistry, biology, business, chemistry, communications, computer science and information, economics, education, English, fine arts, food science and technology, history, home economics, horticulture, journalism, mathematics, medical technology, music, natural science, psychology, religion, social science and theology.

FEES

Cost per academic year: tuition, room and board $8000.

DISTINGUISHED ALUMNI

Dr. Benjamin F. Reaves	-	An alumnus who became Oakwood College President
Lloyd B. Mallory	-	Concert Director Lincoln University (PA)
Dr. Thelma D. Anderson	-	Chairperson, Business Dept. Albany State College
Ina M. Boon	-	Former Director, NAACP Region IV
Witley A. Phipps	-	Pastor, Capitol Hill S.D.A. Church, Washington, D.C.

SELMA UNIVERSITY

Selma University, originally established in 1878 and affiliated with the Baptist Church, trained Colored youth for religious service. Under the leadership of Ms. A. Stone, the Women's Baptist State Convention erected the first girls' dormitory and provided access to academic training for female students in the Black Belt region.

CHRONOLOGY OF NAME CHANGES

1878	-	Selma University
1881	-	Alabama Baptist Colored University
1908	-	Selma University

LOCATION

The campus is located approximately forty-five miles west of Montgomery and within walking distance to the nearby shopping center. Proximity to Montgomery makes for easy access to and from the campus. The major transportation is by Trailway Bus and private car.

The Address: **Selma University**
                  Selma, Alabama 36701
                  Telephone: (205) 872-2533

THE INSTITUTION

Average enrollment at the college is 200 with dormitories available on a first-come first-served basis. Each student is assigned by the Academic Dean to a faculty advisor who will assist the student in registration and planning a program of study relevant to the student's career goals. To qualify for the baccalaureate degree, the student must complete the general education curriculum (50 semester credit hours). The core curriculum is designed to develop values, skills and attitudes in students which will equip them to compete in today's society. The university is divided into the following academic divisions:

- Business, Computer Science and Mathematics
- Health, Physical Education and Recreation
- Humanities and Social Sciences
- Natural Sciences
- Religion

The college offers the Bachelor of Arts in Religion and the Bachelor of Science in Biology, Business Administration and Management Information Systems. The Associate of Arts degree is also offered in a variety of fields.

FEES

Cost per academic year: tuition, room and board $5000.

DISTINGUISHED ALMUNI

| Burnest Webster Dawson | - | President Selma University |
| Alvin A. Cleveland, Sr. | - | Religion Professor Selma University |

STILLMAN COLLEGE

Stillman College is a private school affiliated with the Presbyterian Church. Established in 1876 as a school to train ministers, it became a junior college in 1937 and a four-year institution in 1948. The college awarded its first baccalaureate in 1951.

CHRONOLOGY OF NAME CHANGES

1876 - Tuscaloosa Institute
1895 - Stillman Institute
1948 - Stillman College

LOCATION

The one-hundred-acre campus is located forty-five minutes southwest of Birmingham, the largest city in the state and steel capital of the South. Proximity to Birmingham makes for ease of transportation to and from the campus.

The Address: **Stillman College
P.O. Box Drawer 1430
Tuscaloosa, Alabama 35403
Telephone: (205) 349-4240**

INSTITUTION

The average enrollment at the college is 700 and the student/faculty ratio is fifteen-to-one. On-campus housing is available. A bachelor's degree is awarded in the following areas: biology, business administration, chemistry, communications, computer science, education, engineering, English, health and physical education, history, mathematics, music, physics, religion and sociology.

FEES

Cost per academic year: tuition $3000, room and board $2500.

DISTINGUISHED ALUMNI

Dr. Alex A. Chambers	-	President, Lane College
Raymond C. Brown	-	Director of Admissions
		Selma University
Sabado Benito	-	Professor of English
		Rust College

TALLADEGA COLLEGE

Talladega college is a private school affiliated with the United Church of Christ. It was founded in 1867 by the American Missionary Association and originally established as a primary school. It was incorporated in 1869 and chartered in 1889. The first instruction at the postsecondary level was in 1890 and the first baccalaureate degree was awarded in 1895.

LOCATION

The 430-acre campus is situated between Atlanta (seventy-five miles east) and Birmingham (40 miles west). Talladega is accessible by bus, passenger rail service and private car.

The Address: **Talladega College**
627 West Battle Street
Talladega, Alabama 35160
Telephone: (205) 362-0206
1-800-633-2440

THE INSTITUTION

Talladega has an average enrollment of approximately 750 and a student/faculty ratio of twelve-to-one. On-campus housing is available. The following programs are available for selection as the major area of study: biology, business administration, chemistry, communications, computer science, economics, education, English, foreign language, history, language, mathematics, music, physical education, physics, psychology, public administration, rehabilitation services, social welfare work, and sociology.

Dual-degree programs are available in: biomedical science with Meharry Medical College, engineering with Auburn University, engineering and veterinary medicine with Tuskegee University, and pharmacy with Florida Agricultural and Mechanical University.

FEES

Cost per academic year: tuition $3500, room and board $2700.

DISTINGUISHED ALUMNI

Jewel Plummer Cobb	-	Former President, California State University, Fullerton
Ruth Simm Hamilton	-	Professor, Michigan State University Trustee - T I A A
Dr. William R. Harvey	-	President, Hampton Univ.
Aaron Brown	-	President emeritus Albany State
Margaret B. Wilson Esq.	-	Asst. Attorney General Missouri
Alberta Helyn Johnson	-	First African-American woman elected to public office in Wyoming.

TUSKEGEE UNIVERSITY

Tuskegee is a private, independent institution founded in 1881 by Booker T. Washington. The first instruction at the postsecondary level was offered in 1923 and the first baccalaureate degree was awarded in 1925. The founder of the United Negro College Fund (UNCF) was Dr. Frederick D. Patterson, third president of Tuskegee University.

CHRONOLOGY OF NAME CHANGES

1881 - Tuskegee Normal and Industrial Institute
1937 - Tuskegee Institute
1986 - Tuskegee University

LOCATION

Tuskegee is located 40 miles east of Montgomery, 75 miles south of Birmingham and 135 miles northeast of Atlanta. The campus is accessible by bus and car. Most students fly into either Montgomery or Atlanta and use automobile transportation to the campus.

The Address: **Tuskegee University**
Tuskegee, Alabama 36088
Telephone: (205) 727-8500

THE INSTITUTION

Tuskegee is one of the best known historically black colleges. It was the first black institution to be declared a National Historic Landmark and is the only "living" college campus designated a National Historic Site and District by Congress. Much of the two-hundred-acre campus was built by former slaves. The university has an average enrollment of 3000 students. On-campus residence halls house fifty-one percent of the student body and housing is available for married students. Both Army and Air Force ROTC programs thrive here. It was the first site for the training of black military pilots and has more graduates who became flag officers than any other institution. Tuskegee established the first nursing degree in Alabama. The school has a student/faculty ratio of fifteen-to-one.

Dual-degree programs are offered with several colleges including Bethune-Cookman College, College of the Virgin Islands, Stillman College and Rust College. A cooperative bachelor degree is offered in forestry with Auburn University, Iowa State University, N.C. State University at Raleigh, University of Michigan, Virginia Polytechnic Institute and State University.

Degrees are offered in accounting, agribusiness, aerospace science, animal science, biology, building construction, business administration, chemistry, computer science, counseling/student personnel, economics, education, engineering, English, food science and technology, history, home economics, industrial arts, mathematics, medical technology, nursing, occupational therapy, physical education, physics, plant and soil science, political science, psychology, radiology technology, social welfare work, sociology and veterinary medicine.

The strongest programs are in engineering, aerospace science and veterinary medicine, which offers a combined Bachelor's/Doctoral program.

FEES

Cost per academic semester: tuition $2900, room and board, $1400.

DISTINGUISHED ALUMNI

Ralph Waldo Ellison	-	Novelist, Invisible Man & other works
Chappie James	-	First Four-Star General
Herman Jerome Russell	-	Millionaire Builder/ Land Developer
Lionel Brockman Richie	-	Muscian
Keenan Ivory Wayans	-	TV Actor/Producer
William Dawson	-	Internationally known Muscian/Composer/ Conductor
Arthur W. Mitchell	-	First Black Democrat ever elected to serve in the U.S. Congress
Dr. Billy C. Black	-	President, Albany State
Elizabeth E. Wright	-	Founder, Voorhees College
Dr. Matthew Jenkins	-	CEO SDD Enterprises Inc. Entrepreneur/Philanthropist

3 H/PBCUs

ARKANSAS BAPTIST COLLEGE

Arkansas Baptist College is a private institution affiliated with the Arkansas Consolidated Baptist Convention. It was established in 1884. The first instruction at the baccalaureate level began near the turn of the century.

<u>LOCATION</u>

The college is located in Little Rock, the state capital and largest city. The city offers a fascinating blend of ante-bellum homes and modern metropolitan buildings. Available relatively close to the campus one can find shopping centers, restaurants and a variety of churches. Transportation to the campus is available by bus system, passenger rail service and air travel.

The Address: **Arkansas Baptist College**
1600 Bishop Street
Little Rock, Arkansas 72202
Telephone: (501) 374-7856

THE INSTITUTION

Arkansas Baptist is a small college with an enrollment of less than 500 and a student/faculty ratio of sixteen-to-one. On-campus housing is available on a first-come first-served basis. The college offers an interdisciplinary program in general studies and awards the baccalaureate degree in business administration, computer science, education, religion, social science and social work.

Each year, in July, the college choir performs in the Los Angeles area.

FEES

Cost per academic year: tuition, room and board : $6000.

DISTINGUISHED ALUMNI

Dr. Odelle Jonas - Vice President, Baptist Congress of Michigan

Dr. Emeral Cosby - Principal, Persing High School Detroit

Hosea Franklin - Associate Professor LeMoyne-Owen College

PHILANDER SMITH COLLEGE

Established as a seminary, Philander is a private, independent institution affiliated with the United Methodist Church. The first postsecondary instruction was offered in 1877. The school was chartered in 1883 and awarded the first bachelor's degree in 1888.

CHRONOLOGY OF NAME CHANGES

1877 - Walden Seminary
1882 - Philander Smith College

LOCATION

Philander Smith College is located in Little Rock which is the capital, the largest city and the geographical center of the state of Arkansas. The college's twenty-acre campus is in the heart of the downtown area. It is served by mass transit bus system, an airport eight miles from the campus and passenger rail service less than three miles from campus.

The Address: **Philander Smith College**
812 West 13th Street
Little Rock, Arkansas 72202
Telephone: (501) 375-9845

THE INSTITUTION

With an enrollment averaging 500, a student/faculty ratio of ten-to-one, Philander Smith College offers small, personal classes with concerned instructors. On-campus residence halls house 17 percent of the student body. The academic programs are divided into five basic areas:
- Business and Economics
- Education
- Humanities
- Natural and Physical Science
- Social Science

A baccalaureate degree is awarded in biology, business administration, chemistry, education, English, mass communication, health, physical education and recreation, home economics, mathematics, medical technology, philosophy and religion, political science, psychology, secretarial science, social work and sociology. Additionally, a dual-degree program in engineering with Tuskegee University is available.

FEES

Cost per academic year: tuition $2500, room and board, $2200.

DISTINGUISHED ALUMNI

Ozell Sutton	-	Past National President of Alpha Phi Alpha Fraternity
Eddie Reed, M.D.	-	Cancer Research Scientist
Lottie Shackleford	-	First Female Mayor of Little Rock, Arkansas
Leslie T. Rogers	-	Associate Professor, Rust College
Sherman E. Tate	-	Vice President, Consumer & Community Affairs, Arkansas Louisiana Gas Co.
Carl Gordon Harris	-	Department Head Norfolk State

UNIVERSITY OF ARKANSAS
AT PINE BLUFF

First instruction at the postsecondary level was offered in 1875. The first baccalaureate degree was awarded in 1882. The institute became a junior college in 1885, a senior college in 1929, and merged with University of Arkansas in 1972.

CHRONOLOGY OF NAME CHANGES

1875 - Branch Normal College
1928 - Arkansas Argricultural, Mechanical and Normal College
1972 - University of Arkansas at Pine Bluff

LOCATION

Located in southeast Arkansas, the campus is approximately thirty-five miles from Little Rock, the capital and largest city in the state. Access to the campus is easy because of the proximity to the capital. A mass transit bus system and the airport serve the needs of the campus.

The Address: **University of Arkansas, Pine Bluff**
North Cedar Street
Pine Bluff, Arkansas 71601
Telephone: (501) 541-6500

THE INSTITUTION

This nearly three-hundred-acre campus is the largest institution of higher learning in southeast. Arkansas. The total campus is 754 acres, with approximately 450 acres used for agricultural research and demonstration farming.

Enrollment at the college averages 3000. On-campus housing is available.

Degrees are offered in accounting, agriculture, astronomy, animal science, anthropology, art/advertising, biology, business administration, business education, chemistry, child/family development, communication, community development, computer science, criminal justice, drama, economics, education, English, fire control and safety, fisher biology, food science and technology, foreign language, health and physical education, history home economics, industrial arts, mathematics, mechanics, music, nursing, personnel administration, physics, political science, psychology, social science and technical teacher training.

FEES

Cost per academic year: tuition $3000, room and board $2500.

DISTINGUISHED ALUMNI

Dr. William T. Keaton	-	President, Arkansas Baptist
Dr. Herbert Carter	-	Vice Chancellor University of California Los Angeles
Edna M. Douglas	-	Past Grand Basileus Sigma Gamma Rho Sorority
Charles Marshall	-	Professor of Business Lane College
Dr. H. Beecher Hicks Jr.	-	Senior Minister Metropolitan Baptist Church Washington, D.C.

California

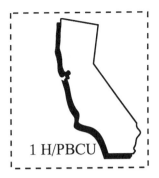

1 H/PBCU

CHARLES R. DREW UNIVERSITY OF MEDICINE AND SCIENCE

The University is named in honor of an outstanding African-American surgeon, Charles R. Drew M.D. It was chartered in 1966 as a private non-profit educational institution. It is the only minority-focused educational center west of the Mississippi, the only minority-focused health science institution on the west coast, and one of four minority medical schools in the United States. In 1983, the university established the College of Allied Health. The first class of Physician Assistant students received the Bachelor of Science degree in June, 1988.

LOCATION

Charles Drew is located in south-central Los Angeles. Easy access to the campus is available due to its proximity to the city of Los Angeles. Airports in Los Angeles, Long Beach and Santa Ana offer a variety of options for reaching the campus for students from out of the area. In addition to a municipal bus system that runs regularly near the campus, a newly opened metro line (Blue Line) is within two blocks of the campus.

The Address: **Charles R. Drew University**
1621 E. 120th Street
Los Angeles, California 90059
Telephone: (213) 563-5851

THE INSTITUTION

The private co-educational institution was created to train persons to provide care to underserved populations. In 1978, the school entered into an affiliation agreement with the University of California to provide education leading to the M.D. degree. The undergraduate medical education program began in the fall of 1981. The first two years of the Drew/UCLA program are spent at UCLA and the last two years are spent at the King/Drew Medical Center. The school enrolls a maximum of twenty-four persons per year.

At the university is the College of Medicine, the College of Allied Health, a learning resource center, a center for community and preventive medicine, an international health institute, a Medical Magnet high school and 17 Drew Head Start centers. There is also an extensive research center, as well as nearly 30 community programs addressing teenage pregnancy, AIDS, cancer, family planning, neuroscience, alcoholism and geriatrics.

FEES

Cost per academic semester: tuition $800.

DISTINGUISHED ALUMNI/STAFF

Dr. David Satcher   -   President
Meharry Medical College

Delaware

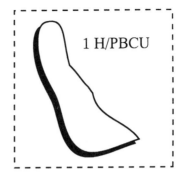

1 H/PBCU

DELAWARE STATE COLLEGE

Delaware State, a state-supported co-educational institution, was founded in 1891. It was started as an institution to train the Colored students of Delaware. The first instruction at the postsecondary level was in held in 1892; the first baccalaureate degree was awarded in 1893.

CHRONOLOGY OF NAME CHANGES

     1891 -   State College for Colored Students
     1947 -   Delaware State College

LOCATION

Delaware State College can be found in the capital city of Dover which is located in the central part of Delaware. Students have use of many modes of transportation as well as easy access to water and water sports on Delaware Bay. Transportation to and from the campus is made easy by the city bus system; also available are passenger rail service and air transportation.

The Address: **Delaware State College**
1200 North Dupoint Highway
Dover, Delaware, 19901
Telephone: (302) 739-4914

THE INSTITUTION

The state-supported liberal arts college is located on 400 acres near the state capitol. There is limited housing available on a first-come basis for the nearly 2500 students.

There is a wide selection of undergraduate major fields and a variety of courses in other disciplines offered by the college. The major departments are Agriculture and Natural Resources, Airway Science, Art and Art Education, Biology, Chemistry, English, Cooperative Engineering Program, Economics and Business Administration, Education, Foreign Language, Health, Physical Education, History and Political Science, Home Economics, Mathematics, Music, Nursing, Psychology, Social Work and Sociology. A dual-degree program is available in engineering with the University of Delaware.

The college offers the associate, the bachelor's and the master's degrees and has a faculty/student ratio of fourteen-to-one.

FEES

Cost per academic year: tuition, room and board $5200.

DISTINGUISHED ALUMNI

Denise M. Gaither-Hardy - Asst. Vice President
Academic Affairs
Lincoln University (PA)
Wayne Gilchrest - U.S. Representative,
1st District, Chestertown, MD
United States Congress

2 H/PBCUs

HOWARD UNIVERSITY

Howard was founded as a private university in 1867 by an Act of the U.S. Congress. The university was named after General Otis Howard, Commissioner of the Freedmen's Bureau. The university has been coeducational as well as multiracial since its first year of operations. Howard offered its first instruction at the postsecondary level in 1867; the first baccalaureate degree was awarded in 1872.

LOCATION

The main campus of 89 acres campus sits on a hill in northwest Washington, D.C., overlooking the downtown area. Located in the nation's capital, Howard provides a stimulating learning environment. Access to the White House, Library of Congress (largest library in the world), the State Treasury, the Pentagon and other government offices are among the many resources available to students who select Howard.

The campus is served by mass transit bus and subway systems. The airport is six miles from campus and passenger rail service is two miles from campus.

The Address: **Howard University**
2400 Sixth Street, NW
Washington, D.C. 20059-0001
Telephone: (202) 806-6100

THE INSTITUTION

Howard is a private, co-educational institution with an enrollment
that averages 12,5000 students (slightly more women than men).
On-campus residences house 30 percent of the student body.

The academic program is divided into schools and colleges. These
are:

- College of Allied Health
- College of Dentistry

- College of Fine Arts
- College of Liberal Arts
- College of Medicine
- College of Nursing
- College of Pharmacy and
  Pharmaceutical Sciences

- School of Architecture
- School of Business and Public
  Administration
- School of Communication
- School of Education
- School of Engineering
- School of Human Ecology
- School of Social Work
- School of Theology

The student/faculty ratio is ten-to-one. Advanced placement for
postsecondary-level work and for extra-institutional learning (life
experience) is an option with evaluation based on the ACE Military
Guide, portfolio, faculty assessment and personal interviews. Student
exchange programs and cross-registration are available with a wide
range of institutions across the United States. The university awards
the following: Baccalaureate; First Professional degree in Dentistry,
Law, Medicine and Theology; Master's and Doctorate.
Intercollegiate athletics are available for men and women. The
university is a level-one ranked research institution, one of only 70
such institutions in the United States.

FEES

Cost per academic year: tuition $5500, room and board $5000.

DISTINGUISHED ALUMNI

Patricia Roberts Harris	-	U.S. Secretary of HUD and first African-American woman to be a member of the President's cabinet.
Edward W. Brooke	-	First African-American Senator in the 20th Century.
Christopher Edley	-	Former President/CEO UNCF
Ossie Davis	-	Actor
David Dinkins	-	Mayor, New York City
Jimmie Johnson	-	Washington Redskins
Mary Frances Berry	-	Former Asst. Secretary of Education U.S. Dept. of Health, Education and Welfare
Alain Locke	-	1st Black Rhodes Scholar
Dr. Paul W. Smith	-	President, Physicians Relations Providence Hospital, D.C.
Melvin Evans	-	1st Elected Governor of the United States Virgin Islands
Joseph T. McMillan	-	President Huston-Tillotson College
Trudy Haynes	-	Reporter, KYN-TV

UNIVERSITY OF
THE DISTRICT OF COLUMBIA

The University is a federal institution and land-grant college comprising three separately accredited campuses: Georgia/Harvard campus, Mount Vernon Square Campus and Van Ness campus. It was established in 1976 as the result of a merger of District of Columbia Teachers College (established 1851), Federal City College (established 1966) and Washington Technical College (established 1966). The first instruction at the postsecondary level was in 1977 and the first baccalaureate degree was awarded in 1978.

LOCATION

The University of the District of Columbia (UDC) is located near the nation's capitol. It is served by mass transit, bus, an airport fifteen miles from campus, passenger rail service ten miles from campus and an extensive taxi service.

The Address: **University of the District of Columbia**
4200 Connneticut Avenue
Washington, D.C. 20008
Telephone: (202) 282-7300

THE INSTITUTION

The University is a co-educational, urban institution that emphasizes preparation for education professions. The enrollment averages 11,000 and there is no on-campus housing. The student/faculty ratio is twenty-to-one. Intercollegiate athletics are an option in basketball, tennis and track for both men and women.

Degrees are awarded in the following areas: accounting, administration and supervision, airway science, architecture, audiology, biological science, building construction, business, chemistry, city planning, communication, computer science, counseling/student personnel, criminal justice, curriculum & instruction, drama, earth science, economics, education, engineering, English, foreign language, geography, health and physical education, history, home economics, horticulture, industrial arts, labor studies, library science, mathematics, mental health, music, nursing, philosophy, physics, political science, print management, procurement/public contract, public policy, reading, religion, social sciences, special education, speech and language pathology, and urban planning.

FEES

Cost per academic year: tuition $3000.

DISTINGUISHED ALUMNI

Floretta Duke McKenzie	-	Former Deputy Asst. Secretary-Dept. of Education 1982-Superintendent, D.C. Public Schools
Joyce F. Leland	-	Deputy Chief of Police Metropolitian Police Dept. Washington, D.C.
Marian Johnson-Thompson	-	Molecular Virologist

Florida

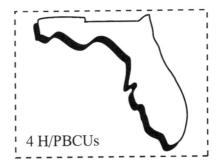

4 H/PBCUs

BETHUNE-COOKMAN COLLEGE

Bethune-Cookman college began as two separate institutions, one that started in 1872 (Daytona-Cookman) and a second in 1904 (Daytona Institute for Girls). In 1923 the charter was issued and the school was established as Daytona-Cookman Collegiate Institute. The first postsecondary instruction was offered in 1932. The upper division curriculum was added in 1941 and the first baccalaureate degree was awarded in 1943. In 1931, the name of the college was changed to include "Bethune", with reference to Mary McLeod Bethune an African American educator who served as an advisor on minority affairs for President Franklin D. Roosevelt. The college is affiliated with the United Methodist Church.

CHRONOLOGY OF NAME CHANGES

1872	-	Cookman Institute
1904	-	Daytona Normal and Industrial Institute for Girls
1923	-	Daytona-Cookman Collegiate Institute
1931	-	Bethune-Cookman College

LOCATION

The college is located in Daytona Beach, one of the popular beach cities of Florida. It is approximately 200 miles east of the capital, Tallahassee, and slightly more than 200 miles north of the largest city, Miami.

The Address: **Bethune-Cookman College**
640 Second Avenue
Daytona Beach, Florida 32074
Telephone: (904) 255-1401

THE INSTITUTION

Bethune-Cookman is a private, liberal arts college with an average enrollment of 2300 and a student/faculty ratio of fifteen-to-one. The forty-five-acre site provides housing for sixty-one percent of the student body. The baccalaureate degree is granted in the following areas: business, education, humanities, science and mathematics, and social sciences. Opportunities are also available to participate in dual-degree programs with Tuskegee University and University of Florida.

FEES

Cost per academic year: tuition, room and board $6000.

DISTINGUISHED ALUMNI

Dr. Alfred S. Smith   -   Asst. Vice President
Academic Affairs
Alabama State University
Sadye Martin   -   Mayor, Plant City, FL

EDWARD WATERS COLLEGE

The College was founded in 1866. It is affiliated with the African Methodist Episcopal Church and was among the first institutions specifically established to educate Blacks for the clergy. It was also the first Black institution in Florida.

CHRONOLOGY OF NAME CHANGES

1866 - Brown Theological Institution
1874 - Brown University
1891 - Edward Waters College

LOCATION

The twenty-acre campus is located in Jacksonville, the third largest city in Florida. The city is less than 20 miles from the Georgia state line. Located near the mouth of the St. Johns River, Jacksonville is a great ship port and yacht harbor. The campus is served by the mass transit bus system, with the airport approximately 15 miles from campus and passenger rail service three miles from campus.

The Address: **Edward Waters College**
1658 Kings Road
Jacksonville, Florida 32209
Telephone: (904) 355-3030

THE INSTITUTION

The Institution is small, private, co-educational and affiliated with the African Methodist Episcopal Church. It offers a baccalaureate degree in more than 15 majors including accounting, airway science, biology, business administration, chemistry, communications, criminal justice, education, health and physical education, mathematics, philosophy, psychology, religion, and sociology. Joint programs have been established with the University of North Florida. Housing is available on a first-come first-served basis for approximately18 percent of the student body. The student/faculty ratio is approximately fifteen-to-one.

FEES

Cost per academic year: tuition, room and board $4000.

DISTINGUISHED ALUMNI

Dr. Lawrence Callahan	-	Founder and Manager of five interdenominational churches in Florida and the Bahamas
Dr. Frederick Harper	-	Publisher, Faculty Member Howard University
William Roberts	-	Attorney-at-Law Jacksonville, Florida
John Robinson	-	President, Robinson's Marketing Co.

FLORIDA AGRICULTURAL
AND MECHANICAL UNIVERSITY

Established as a state college for Colored students in 1887, the first instruction at the postsecondary level began in 1905. The first baccalaureate was awarded in 1910.

The doors of the college were opened with two instructors and 15 students. It was designated a land-grant institution in 1890 and became a university in 1953.

CHRONOLOGY OF NAME CHANGES

    1887 - The State Normal College for Colored Students
    1909 - Florida Agricultural and Mechanical College
    1953 - Florida Agricultural and Mechanical University

LOCATION

The University (called FAMU) is located on the highest of seven hills in Tallahassee (population over 140,000) and approximately twenty-two miles from the Gulf of Mexico. There are more than 1000 acres of public parks and land and numerous lakes nearby. It is located eight blocks from the Capitol Complex. Bus service is available from campus to recreational areas, shopping malls, state, county and city offices. There is also an inter-campus shuttle and a daily on-campus shuttle which runs during class hours.

The FAMU campus—covered by lush shrubbery, flowering plants, and massive oaks—has 108 buildings spread across 419 acres.

The Address: **Florida Agricultural and Mechanical University**
1500 Wahnish Way
Tallahassee, Florida 32307
Telephone: (904) 599-3796

THE INSTITUTION

Florida A & M University (FAMU), has an average student body population of 7200 and a student/faculty ratio of eighteen-to-one. On-campus housing, available for single and married students, is provided on a first-come first-served basis. There are more than 100 student organizations on campus. This includes nationally affiliated fraternities and sororities, honor societies, religious groups, Orchesis Contemporary Dance Theater, the Playmakers Guild, the FAMU Gospel Choir and the famed Marching One Hundred.

FAMU's 282-member marching band has received national television and magazine coverage and was the first band outside the Big 10 Conference to earn the Sousa Foundation's prestigious Sudler Trophy.

FAMU has been noted for its athletic facilities which include Bragg Stadium (25,000 capacity) with a field house, locker rooms, weight room and training facility; a track and field complex with an eight-lane, all weather, four-hundred-meter track; competition grade tennis courts; two outdoor pools; baseball and softball fields; and a complex that serves as headquarters for the largest women's athletic program at any historically black institution in the country.

In 1991, FAMU enrolled more National Achievement Scholars than any other school except Harvard.

The University awards the associate, the baccalaureate, the master's and the first professional (pharmacy) degrees. The major academic areas are:

- The College of Arts and Science
- The College of Education
- The College of Engineering Sciences, Technology and Agriculture
- The School of Pharmacy and Pharmaceutical Sciences
- The School of Architecture
- The School of Business and Industry (SBI)
- The School of Journalism, Media, and Graphic Arts
- The School of Nursing
- The School of General Studies which facilitates and monitors the general education of all matriculating students.

Off-campus and joint arrangements are available in Washington, D.C., Miami and other parts of the continental United States, and with Florida State University. Students have interned in such places as England, Puerto Rico, Australia and Switzerland.

FEES

Cost per academic semester: tuition $1500, room and board $1200-$1500.

DISTINGUISHED ALUMNI

Nat "Cannon Ball" Adderley	-	Musician
Willie Galemore, Althea Gibson	-	Athletes
Frederick S. Humphries	-	8th President, FAMU
Joseph W. Hatchett	-	U.S. Circuit Judge 5th Circuit, Tallahassee, FL
Rev. Cecil Murray	-	Sr. Minister, First AME Church, Los Angeles, CA

FLORIDA MEMORIAL COLLEGE

The College was established in 1879 as Florida Baptist Institute. A merger of Florida Baptist Institute and Florida Normal and Industrial School resulted in Florida Baptist Academy. The first instruction at the postsecondary level was offered in 1918. In 1945, the first baccalaureate was awarded.

CHRONOLOGY OF NAME CHANGES

1879	-	Florida Baptist Institute for Negroes
1892	-	Florida Normal and Industrial School
1917	-	Florida Baptist Academy
1918	-	Florida Normal and Industrial Institute
1950	-	Florida Normal and Industrial Memorial College
1963	-	Florida Memorial College

LOCATION

The seventy-two-acre campus is located in cosmopolitan Miami, the largest city in Florida. The campus enjoys the benefits of transportation and the recreational centers associated with this resort city. Mass transit bus service is available to the recreational areas, the shopping malls and the various libraries and other municipal service areas. It is the only Black college in the southern portion of the state.

The Address: **Florida Memorial College**
15800 Northwest 42nd Avenue
Miami, Florida 33054
Telephone: (305) 625-4141

INSTITUTION

Florida Memorial is a private, co-educational college affiliated with the Baptist Church. The college has an average enrollment of 1800 students with a student/faculty ratio of thirty-to-one. On campus housing is available for approximately 70 percent of the student body.

Advanced placement for postsecondary-level work completed in secondary school and for extra-institutional (life) experience is evaluated on the basis of portfolio, faculty assessments and personal interviews. Weekly chapel is a requirement.

The baccalaureate degree is awarded in the following areas: accounting, airway science management, biology, business management, chemistry, computer science, economics, education, English, health and physical education, mathematics, music, philosophy, physics, political science, psychology, public affairs, religion, social science, transportation management, and visual and performing arts.

FEES

Cost per academic year: tuition $3000, room and board $2700.

DISTINGUISHED ALUMNI

Nelis J. Saunders   -   Former Michigan
                          Legislator, 11th District

Georgia

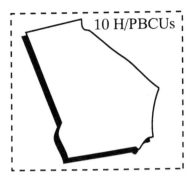

10 H/PBCUs

ALBANY STATE COLLEGE

Albany State was founded in 1903 by Joseph Wintrop Holly. The institution provided religious and manual training for Black youth of southwestern Georgia. The mission was to train teachers to teach basic academic skills and to train in the trades and industries, with special emphasis on domestic science and art. In 1932, the Board of Regents was established and the institution became part of the University System of Georgia. Albany State College is a state-supported co-educational institution.

CHRONOLOGY OF NAME CHANGES

1903	-	Albany Bible and Manual Training Institute
1917	-	Georgia Normal and Agricultural College
1943	-	Albany State College

LOCATION

Atlanta, the nearest metropolitan area is one-hundred-and-forty-five miles from the campus. The nearest airport is in Albany, five miles from campus. Information about the college can be obtained by writing or calling:

The Address: **Albany State College**
504 College Drive
Albany, Georgia 31705
Telephone: (912) 430-4600 and 430-4604

Transportation to and from the campus is available by the public bus transit system. Most of the major airlines service the Atlanta area. Passenger rail service is also available.

THE INSTITUTION

Albany State is a liberal arts college with an enrollment of approximately 2500 students. The student/faculty ratio is fourteen-to-one. The institution has been in a constant mode of change. In 1943 the college was granted a four-year status and was authorized to confer the bachelor's degree in elementary education and home economics. In 1954 the secondary level programs were developed for teacher preparation in science, health and physical education, business, music, mathematics, and natural science. In 1961 the college was authorized to offer a four-year degree program in nursing. Today, the college provides instructional programs in the following areas:

SCHOOL OF ARTS AND SCIENCES
- Department of Criminal Justice
- Department of Developmental Studies
- Department of English and Modern Languages
- Department of Fine Arts
- Department of History and Political Science
- Department of Mathematics and Computer Science
- Department of Natural Science
- Department of Psychology, Sociology, and Social Work

SCHOOL OF BUSINESS
- Department of Business Administration
- Department of Business Education and Office Administration

SCHOOL OF EDUCATION
- Department of Curriculum and Instruction
- Department of Health and Physical Education

SCHOOL OF NURSING AND ALLIED HEALTH
- Department of Nursing
- Department of Allied Health

GRADUATE SCHOOL PROGRAMS
- Department of Education
- Department of Business Administration
- Department of Criminal Justice

FEES

The fiscal year for the College consists of four quarters - summer, fall, winter and spring. Cost per academic quarter: tuition, room and board $2500. Students from outside the Albany area are expected to live on the campus.

DISTINGUISHED ALUMNI

Evelyn A. Hodge	-	Reading Supervisor Alabama State University
Alice Coachman Davis	-	First Black Olympics Gold Medalist, Women's Track and Field
William A. Hopkins	-	Director-Small Business Affairs, Georgia
William A. Johnson	-	Vice President, Fiscal Affairs, Albany State

THE ATLANTA CENTER

The largest cluster of private Black institutions of higher education in the world is the Atlanta University Center System (AUC). The Center is an association of seven institutions - four undergraduate colleges and three graduate institutions on adjoining campuses in the center of Atlanta.

The undergraduate schools are:
Clark Atlanta University
Morehouse College
Morris Brown College
Spelman College

The graduate schools are:
Clark Atlanta University
Morehouse College of Medicine
The Interdenominational Theological Seminary
(a federation of six Protestant seminaries)

All seven schools share a number of academic facilities and are closely linked socially. Cross-registration is enjoyed by all. Each institution remains independent, each with its own administration, board of trustees and academic specialities and each maintains its own dormitories, cafeterias and other facilities. There is a center-wide dual-degree program in engineering with Georgia Institute of Technology. The Center also sponsors career planning and placement where recruiters may come and interview students from the Center institutions.

Morehouse, an all-male college, and Spelman, a women's college, maintain a close academic and social relationship. The Christmas concert by the Morehouse-Spelman Glee Club is a highlight of the seasonal festivities.

The governing body of the consortium is the Atlanta University Center, Inc. Two trustees from each of the schools sit on its board along with outside members.

Located in the New South, the AUC is viewed as a preeminent location in the country for bright, talented, and successful African-Americans. It is the home to some of the most respected and well-known Black politicians and business people.

Students enrolled at AUC institutions have the opportunity to hear a world-class symphony orchestra, to view a renowned ballet company, to visit art museums and galleries, and to dine in splendid restaurants. The city is also the home of the Martin Luther King, Jr. Center for Non-Violent Social Change and the Jimmy Carter Presidential Library.

CLARK ATLANTA UNIVERSITY

Clark College was founded in 1869 by the Freedmen's Aid Society of the Methodist Episcopal Church for the purpose of providing Blacks in the South with a formal education.

The institution was organized as Clark University and chartered by the state of Georgia in 1877. The name "Clark" was given to the university in honor of Bishop Davis W. Clark, who served as the first president of the Freedmen's Aid Society and worked diligently to build institutions throughout the South to meet the educational needs of Blacks. The first baccalaureate degree was awarded in 1883. In 1988, the Boards of Trustees of Clark College and Atlanta University formally agreed to consolidate the two institutions to form a stronger, more viable institution - Clark Atlanta University.

CHRONOLOGY OF NAME CHANGES

    1869 -   Clark University
    1941 -   Clark College
    1989 -   Clark Atlanta University

LOCATION

One mile east of the Clark College campus are the mirrored sky-scrapers and modern expressways of Atlanta, the Southern metropolis. Served by taxi, bus, and MARTA (Metropolitan Atlanta Rapid Transit), the campus is easily accessible.

The Address: **Clark Atlanta University**
                 240 James P. Brawley Drive, S.W.
                 Atlanta, Georgia 30314
                 Telephone: (404) 681-8017

THE INSTITUTION

Enrollment at this private co-educational institution averages 2000. Clark College is the largest of the seven member Atlanta University Center (AUC). The college owns and operates five residence halls and a 126-unit apartment complex, Clark College Courts. With these facilities, on-campus housing is available to approximately 900 students.

Clark offers two degrees, the Bachelor of Arts (B.A.) and the Bachelor of Science (B.S.) Majors in the B.A. programs include accounting, art, business administration, business education, dramatic arts, economics, education, English, fashion design, history, home economics, human resources development, modern foreign language, mass communications, physical education, political science, psychology, public policy studies, restaurant and institutional management, social science and social welfare.

The B.S. is offered in the following majors: biology, chemistry, clinical dietetics, computer science, engineering (dual-degree program), mathematics, medical illustration, medical records, medical technology, physics, and pre-pharmacy and nutrition.

The college offers the dual-degree in pharmacy with Mercer University and in engineering with Georgia Technological Institute. As a result of the merger with Atlanta University, post baccalaureate options are now available at Clark Atlanta University. The two institutions currently share all resources and facilities.

FEES

Cost per academic year: tuition, room and board $7500.

DISTINGUISHED ALUMNI

Marva Collins   -   Founder and Director, Westside
                            Preparatory School, Chicago

FORT VALLEY STATE COLLEGE

Fort Valley State is a four-year public institution, established initially as Fort Valley High and Industrial School in 1895. In 1939, the school merged with State Teachers and Agriculture College at Forsyth and offered the first instruction at the postsecondary level. The first baccalaureate degree was awarded in 1941.

CHRONOLOGY OF NAME CHANGES

1895	-	Fort Valley High and Industrial School
1932	-	Fort Valley Normal and Industrial School
1939	-	Fort Valley State College

LOCATION

Atlanta, 100 miles away, is the nearest metropolitan area. The campus sits amid six-hundred-and-fifty acres of land in the heart of middle Georgia. The nearest airport is approximately twenty-eight miles from campus.

The Address: **Fort Valley State College**
805 State College Drive
Fort Valley, Georgia 31030
Telephone: (912) 825-6307

THE INSTITUTION

The 660-acre campus area consists of 56 buildings which are an aesthetic blending of stately brick and concrete. The college has an average enrollment of 1800 students with a student/faculty ratio of thirteen-to-one. On campus residence halls house fifty-four percent of the students. Intercollegiate athletics is available in basketball, cross-country, indoor-track, tennis, and track for men and women.

Three schools comprise the academic program at Fort Valley:
- Arts and Science
- Agriculture, Home Economics, and Allied Programs
- Education, Graduate and Special Academic Programs

A dual-degree program is available with Georgia Technology.

Institutionally arranged study abroad is an available option in West Africa and through the University of Georgia at various locations, including Europe. The college is on the quarter system.

FEES

Cost per academic year: tuition $3500, room and board $2500.

DISTINGUISHED ALUMNI

Roy McKenzie	-	Executive Vice President & Co-. Founder, E.A.R. Enterprises
Dr. Cordell Wynn	-	President, Stillman College
Dr. James L. Hill	-	Dean, Albany State College

INTERDENOMINATIONAL THEOLOGICAL CENTER

The Center was founded in 1958 to address the needs for advanced theological education. It is a member of the Atlanta University Center.

The Address: **Interdenominational Theological Center
671 Beckwith Street, SW
Atlanta, Georgia 30314
Telephone: (404) 522-1722**

THE INSTITUTION

The Interdenominational Theological Center is an ecumenical professional graduate school of theology. The constituent seminaries of the Center are Gammon Theological Seminary, Charles H. Mason Theological Seminary, Morehouse School of Religion, Phillips School of Theology, Johnson C. Smith Theological Seminary and Turner Theological Seminary. Six Protestant denominations are represented at the Center: African Methodist Episcopal, Baptist, Christian Methodist Episcopal, Presbyterian (USA), United Methodist, and Church of God in Christ. Enrollment at the Center averages 300 students seeking the first professional degree, the master's and doctorate.

Acceptance at the college requires the bachelor's degree or its equivalent from an accredited college or university and certificate from a major official of the applicant's denomination indicating that the applicant is an acceptable candidate for service in the denomination and that admission to the Center is approved.

Joint enrollment is available with Candler School of Theology of Emory University; Columbia Theological Seminary in Decatur; Erskine Theological Seminary in South Carolina.

Dormitory accommodations as well as efficiency housing and trailers are available on a first-come first-served basis.

The student/faculty ratio is thirteen-to-one.

FEES

Cost per academic year: tuition $2000, room $800, board $1200.

DISTINGUISHED ALUMNI

    Willie Muse   -   Religion Instructor
                          Selma University
    Stevenson E. Tullis -   Religion Instructor
                          Selma University

MOREHOUSE COLLEGE

The college legacy goes back to 1867, when the liberal arts school named after a white missionary was founded in the basement of Springfield Baptist Church to help train newly freed slaves to read and write. Additionally, it planned to prepare Blacks for the ministry and teaching.

CHRONOLOGY OF NAME CHANGES

1867 - Augusta Institute
1879 - Atlanta Baptist Seminary
1897 - Atlanta Baptist College
1945 - Morehouse College

LOCATION

Morehouse is a member of the Atlanta University Center. It is located in Atlanta, the capital and one of the great railroad and banking centers in the United States.

The Address: **Morehouse College**
830 Westview Drive, S.W.
Atlanta, Georgia 30314
Telephone: (404) 681-2800 and 752-1500

THE INSTITUTION

Morehouse is a private independent liberal arts nonprofit college for men. It offers a dual-degree program in engineering with Georgia Institute of Technology as well as a pre-professional program in medicine, interdisciplinary programs in international studies and urban studies. With an average enrollment of 2000 students, the student/faculty ratio is twenty-to-one. On-campus housing can accommodate approximately 40 percent of the student body. Programs available include accounting, business administration, chemistry, child/family development, communication, computer science/information, drama theater, Earth science, economics, education, fine arts, health and physical education, mathematics, music education, natural sciences, political science and government, radio/TV and film, social science, social work, and visual and performing arts.

The Bachelor of Arts and the Bachelor of Science are the degrees awarded upon completion of an academic program.

The college is one of three Black four-year institutions that has a Phi Beta Kappa Chapter.

FEES

Cost per academic year: tuition $4500, room and board $5500.

DISTINGUISHED ALUMNI

Lerone Bennett Jr.	-	Executive Editor Ebony Magazine
Samuel Dubois Cook	-	President Dillard University
Martin Luther King	-	Minister, Civil Rights Activist, Founder SCLC
Spike Lee	-	Film Maker
Andrew Young	-	Former Ambassador to United Nations and Mayor of Atlanta, Georgia
Samuel Nabrit	-	1966, 1st Black member of Atomic Energy Commission

MOREHOUSE SCHOOL OF MEDICINE

Morehouse College spawned a two-year medical education program in 1975. It became an independent, M.D. degree granting institution in 1981. It was the first predominantly Black medical school to be established in the twentieth century. The four-year M.D. granting institution was fully accredited by the Liaison Committee on Medical Education (LCME) in 1985.

LOCATION

The Morehouse School of Medicine is located in Atlanta, Georgia. It is a part of the Atlanta Educational Center. All modes of modern transportation serve the city of Atlanta and it is the hub city for Delta Airlines. Atlanta has more schools dedicated to providing higher education for African-Americans than any other city in the United States.

The Address: **Morehouse School of Medicine**
720 Westview Drive, S.W.
Atlanta, Georgia 30310-1495
Telephone: (404) 752-1500

THE INSTITUTION

The Morehouse School of Medicine is a member of Georgia State University System. The private co-educational institution has an average enrollment of one-hundred-and-thirty students. Approximately 20 students per year are recipients of the First-Professional degree in medicine. The educational program offered by the School of Medicine leads to the degree Doctor of Medicine (M.D.) and focuses on scientific knowledge and meeting the primary health care needs of underserved clients.

FEES

Cost per academic year: tuition $15,000.

DISTINGUISHED ALUMNI/STAFF

Dr. Louis Sullivan   -   Ex-President of the College, Secretary of Health and Human Services in the Cabinet of George Bush.

MORRIS BROWN COLLEGE

A private college affiliated with the African Methodist Episcopal Church, Morris Brown College was established in 1881 as an institution to educate Blacks. It offered the first instruction at the postsecondary level in 1894 and the first baccalaureate degree was awarded in 1898.

CHRONOLOGY OF NAME CHANGES

1881-	-	Morris Brown College
1913	-	Morris Brown University
1929	-	Morris Brown College

LOCATION

Morris Brown is a member of the Atlanta University Center and is located in the Atlanta area.

The Address: **Morris Brown College**
643 Martin Luther King Jr. Dr., S.W.
Atlanta, Georgia 30314
Telephone: (404) 220-0270

THE INSTITUTION

The fifty-two-acre campus has an average enrollment of approximately 1200 students. On-campus residence halls house fifty-five percent of the student body. Intercollegiate athletics are available for men and women. Majors are offered in the following areas: accounting, allied health, biology, business administration, chemistry, computer sciences, criminal justice, economics, education, fashion design/merchandising, hotel and restaurant management, mathematics, music, nursing, physical education, physical therapy, physics, political science and government, psychology, religion, social work, sociology and urban studies.

The dual-degree program in engineering with Georgia Institute of Technology is also available in addition to study abroad in Haiti, Europe, and the Dominican Republic. The student/faculty ratio is fourteen-to-one.

FEES

Cost per academic year: $10,350.

DISTINGUISHED ALUMNI

Dr. Leonard E. Dawson	-	President Voorhees College
Percy J. Vaughn Jr.	-	Dean, College of Business Administration Alabama State University
Beverly J. Harvard	-	1st Woman Deputy of Police in Atlanta Bureau of Police Service
Virgil Hall Hodges	-	Deputy Commissioner NY State Dept. of Labor

PAINE COLLEGE

Paine is a private, liberal arts, coeducational college affiliated with the United Methodist, Christian Methodist Episcopal Church and UNCF. It was established in 1882 to insure the religious education of Black youth. The first postsecondary level instruction was held in 1891; the first baccalaureate degree was awarded in 1895.

CHRONOLOGY OF NAME CHANGES

1882	-	Paine Institute
1903	-	Paine College

LOCATION

Situated between the capitals of Georgia (Atlanta) and South Carolina (Columbia), the college is right at the border of South Carolina. The proximity to two metropolitan areas adds to the options of shopping, concerts, cultural and sporting events. There is easy access to the campus, which is served by a mass transit system and two airports with one being less than ten miles from campus. The city of Augusta also offers choices of concerts and other cultural events.

The Address: **Paine College**
1235 Fifteenth Street
Augusta, Georgia 30910-3182
Telephone: (706) 821-8200
1-800-476-7703

THE INSTITUTION

The average campus enrollment is approximately 700 students. More than half of the students reside on campus. Cross-registration is offered with Augusta College and Clark-Atlanta University.

Degrees are offered in the following areas: biology, business administration, chemistry, education, English, history, mass communications, mathematics, music, psychology, religion, and sociology.

Campus life at Paine affords students the opportunity to participate in numerous clubs, academic and religious, as well as four fraternities and four sororities.

FEES

Cost per academic year: tuition $5200, room $1100, board $1700.

DISTINGUISHED ALUMNI

Frank Yerby -	Author
Dr. Channing H. Tobias -	United Nations Delegate
Dr. William Harris -	President, Texas Southern University
Dr. Shirley McBay -	First minority to serve as Dean of Student Affairs at MIT.
Dr. Morgan C. Brown -	Dean, Bridgewater State College (MA)
Dr. Charles G. Gomillion -	Civil Rights Activist Former Dean, Tuskegee University
Albert Murray -	Former Asst. District Attorney, Kings County. Owner, Hillside Inn, Pocono Mountains

SAVANNAH STATE COLLEGE

The College was established and chartered as a school for Colored youth in 1890. The first instruction at the postsecondary level was in 1926. The first baccalaureate was awarded in 1930.

CHRONOLOGY OF NAME CHANGES

    1890 - Georgia State Industrial College for Colored Youth
    1931 - Georgia State College
    1950 - Savannah State College

LOCATION

The College is in the great export city of Savannah, located on the southeastern part of Georgia, less than five miles from the South Carolina border. All modern modes of transportation are accessible to and from the campus and the students have the opportunity to participate in water sports.

The Address: **Savannah State College**
    P.O Box 20449
    Savannah, Georgia, 31404
    Telephone: (912) 356-2186

THE INSTITUTION

Savannah State College is a senior college of the University System of Georgia. It has an average enrollment of 1900 students and provides housing for 70 percent of the student population. The one-hundred-and-sixty-four-acre campus with 40 buildings has a student/faculty ratio of fifteen-to-one.

The degrees offered include the associate, baccalaureate and the master's. The majors available are: accounting, biology science, business administration, chemical technology, communications, criminal justice/law enforcement, economics, engineering-related technology, English, environmental science, history, humanities, journalism, marine biology, mathematics, medical laboratory technology, music, park and recreation, physics, political science, public administration, recreation/leisure, secretarial science, technology, and urban planning.

FEES

Cost per academic year: tuition $3500, room $1000, board $1500.

DISTINGUISHED ALUMNI

Mayme S. Jeffries	-	Director of Assessment
		Edward Waters College
Mary Dawson Walters	-	1st Black to head one of
		Ohio States' Library Depts.
Helen M. Mayes	-	Director Emerita
		Albany State College

SPELMAN COLLEGE

Spelman has the distinction of being the first Black women's college established in the United States. It is one of only two Black women's colleges in the country. The private liberal arts college was established by the Baptist Church as a seminary for women. The first instruction at the postsecondary level was in 1897 and the first baccalaureate degree was awarded in 1901.

CHRONOLOGY OF NAME CHANGES

    1881 - Atlanta Baptist Female Seminary
    1884 - Spelman Seminary
    1924 - Spelman College

LOCATION

Spelman is a member of the Atlanta University Center. The thirty-two-acre campus is next door to Atlanta's downtown. Access is available to all modern forms of transportation. The hub of Delta's airline operation is Atlanta. Mass transit bus and train systems are readily available. Students attending Spelman have available the most modern shopping malls and entertainment possible.

The Address: **Spelman College**
                    350 Spelman Lane
                    Atlanta, Georgia 30314
                    Telephone: (404) 681-3643

THE INSTITUTION

The college has an average enrollment of 1700 students. On-campus residence halls house sixty-two percent of the student body. Housing is guaranteed to out-of-town freshman. The student/

faculty ratio is twenty-to-one. The baccalaureate degree is awarded in the arts and in the sciences.

Students may select from a variety of majors including: arts and science, biochemistry, biophysics, biology, computer sciences, drama, economics, English, fine arts, history,languages, life science, mathematics, music, philosophy, physical education, political science, pre-medicine, psychology and religion.

The college also offers a dual-degree program in engineering with Georgia Institute of Technology. Cross-registration and co-operative academic programs through the Consortium is also an option.

FEES

Cost per academic year: tuition $4000, room $1800, board $1500.

DISTINGUISHED ALUMNI

Marian W. Edelman J.D. -	Founder Children's Defense Fund and Former Director, Center of Law and Education at Harvard
Ester Rolle -	Actress
Varnette Honeywood -	Artist
Elynor Williams -	Director, Corporate Affairs, Hanes Group, Winston Salem, N.C.
Josephine D. Davis -	Dean, Graduate School Albany State College

Illinois

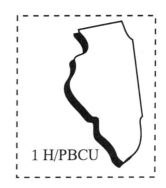

1 H/PBCU

CHICAGO STATE UNIVERSITY

Chicago State University began in a freight car on Blue Island September 2, 1867. It was Cook County's first teacher training school. Having proved that a teacher training school could work, the Cook County Normal School opened September 21, 1870.

CHRONOLOGY OF NAME CHANGES

1870	-	Cook County Normal School
1897	-	Chicago Normal School
1913	-	Chicago Normal College
1938	-	Chicago Teacher's College
1965	-	Illinois Teachers College
1972	-	Chicago State University

LOCATION

Chicago, the great metropolis of the Midwest, is the home of Chicago State University. The university's students are surrounded by many of points of interest, which include Chicago Natural History Museum,

Museum of Science and Industry, Chicago Zoological Park in Brookfield Board of Trade, Prudential Building, Stock Yards and McCormick Place. Identified as having one of the greatest railway centers in the world, and located in the heart of an arterial system, Chicago's transportation system provides easy access to the university.

The Address: **Chicago State University**
95th Street at King Drive
Chicago, Illinois 60628
Telephone: (312) 995-2000

THE INSTITUTION

The 152-acre campus consists of nine buildings: Education; Business and Health Services; Harold Washington Hall; Daniel Hale Williams Science Center; Paul and Emily Douglas Library; Raymond Cook Administration; Physical Education and Athletics; Physical Plant and William H. Robinson University Center.

Enrollment averages 6000 and the university is organized into five colleges. All award the baccalaureate degree:
- College of Allied Health
- College of Arts and Science
- College of Business
- College of Education
- College of Nursing

Over 50 undergraduate and 26 graduate degree programs are offered through the five colleges. The university is organized into four major divisions each administered by a vice-president:

- Academic Affairs
- Administrative Affairs
- Student Affairs
- Institutional Advancement

FEES

Cost per academic year: tuition $5000.

DISTINGUISHED ALUMNI

Edward Gardner	-	Founder and CEO of SoftSheen Products Company
Margaret Burrough	-	Founder/Director Emeritus DuSable Museum of African-American History
Dr. Frank Gardner	-	Board of Examiners Chicago Public Schools
Elizabeth Harris Lawson	-	Co-chair, White House Conf. on Library & Information Services, D.C. 1979

Indiana

1 H/PCBU

MARTIN UNIVERSITY

Martin University, established in 1977, is a private liberal arts institution. It received accreditation as a baccalaureate granting institution in 1986. The university specializes in the advanced academic training of adults.

CHRONOLOGY OF NAME CHANGES

    1977 -   Martin Center College
    1990 -   Martin University

LOCATION

The school is located in the state capital and largest city which lays in the middle of the state. It is a commuter school with bus transportation easily accessible; passenger rail service and air travel offer ready access to the campus.

The Address: **Martin University**
                2171 Avondale Place
                Indianapolis, Indiana 46305
                Telephone: (317) 543-3235

THE INSTITUTION

The student population which averages 700 is more than 90 percent African-American and forty is the average age of students attending the college. The university enjoys a student/faculty ratio of ten-to-one and specializes in accommodating adult learners. The program is student-centered, with each degree individually planned to meet the educational and career goals of the student. The specific degree, i.e. Bachelor of Arts or Bachelor of Science, is determined by the student's overall plan.

The Martin University curriculum is offered by nine academic divisions which include:

- Division of Behavioral Sciences
- Division of Business and Management
- Division of Communication
- Division of Fine Arts
- Division of Global and Environmental Studies
- Division of Humanities
- Division of Justice and Human Rights
- Division of Religious Studies
- Division of Sciences and Mathematics

FEES

The cost to attend the University is dependent upon the number of credit hours selected; the cost per credit hour is $200.

DISTINGUISHED ALUMNI

Grace Robinson　　　-　　Professor, Martin University

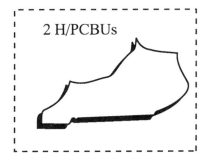

2 H/PCBUs

KENTUCKY STATE UNIVERSITY

Kentucky State is a state-assisted public liberal studies-oriented institution. It was established in 1886 and offered its first instruction at the postsecondary level in 1887. The first baccalaureate was awarded in 1929.

CHRONOLOGY OF NAME CHANGES

    1886 - Kentucky Normal Institute
    1902 - Kentucky Normal and Industrial Institute for Colored Persons
    1926 - Kentucky Industrial College for Colored Persons
    1938 - Kentucky State College for Negroes
    1952 - Kentucky State College
    1972 - Kentucky State University

LOCATION

The University is located in Frankfort, the capital of Kentucky, along the Kentucky River, transportation is readily available to the campus. The city is in the northern tip of Kentucky, approximately

40 miles east of Louisville and the state of Indiana and 50 miles south of Cincinnati, Ohio. The capitol, characteristic of the stately south, houses the Kentucky Historical Society. This is also the burial site of Daniel Boone.

The Address: **Kentucky State University**
East Main Street
Frankfort, Kentucky, 40601
Telephone: (502) 227-6813
1-800-325-1716

THE INSTITUTION

Kentucky State has a student body of approximately 2500 students enrolled in a variey of programs. The college confers the associate, bachelor's, and master's degrees. Non-Kentucky residents, in addition to general requirements, must meet at least one of the following pre-requisites: rank in the upper half of their high school class, score at least the national average on the SAT or demonstrate through other acceptable means the ability to pursue university academic education without substantial remedial aid.

Study programs are available in behavioral and social sciences, business administration, criminal justice, education, fine arts, health and physical education, home economics, humanities, industrial technology, mathematics and science, nursing, public affairs and social work. The student/faculty ratio is nineteen-to-one. On-campus housing is available.

FEES

Cost per academic year: tuition $3200, room $1200, board $1500.

DISTINGUISHED ALUMNI

Ersa H. Poston	-	Former President, New York Civil Services Commission
Whitney Young	-	Leader, National Urban League
Moneta Sleet Jr.	-	Photographer, Johnson Publishing Company
Dr. Rufus Barfield	-	Vice Chancellor University of AR (PB)
Curtis Sullivan	-	President, Omni Custom Meats, Inc.

SIMMONS UNIVERSITY BIBLE COLLEGE

Simmons University Bible College is a small private institution founded in 1897. The original mission was to train preachers and christian educators. It is owned by the General Association of Baptist in Kentucky and offers the Bachelor of Arts and the Bachelor of Theology. The majority of students are over thirty-five and live near the college. There are no dormitory facilities.

LOCATION

The College is located in the largest and most important commercial industrial city in Kentucky. (The home of the Kentucky Derby.) There is a bus transit system, passenger rail service and access to air travel. Transportation to the campus is readily available. It is a commuter school.

The Address: **Simmons University Bible College**
1811 Dumesnil Street
Louisville, Kentucky 40210
Telephone: (502) 776-1443

FEES

The cost is $20 per credit hour and most of the students take nine credit hours per semester.

Louisiana

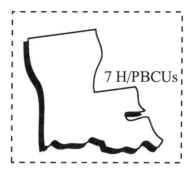

7 H/PBCUs

DILLARD UNIVERSITY

Dillard's history goes back more than a century. Straight College and New Orleans University, the parent institutions, were founded in 1869 and merged in 1930 to form one school named in honor of James Hardy Dillard, a noted scholar and educator. The University is affiliated with the United Church of Christ and the United Methodist Church. Dillard offered the first speech department in a Black university and had the first accredited nursing program in the state of Louisiana.

CHRONOLOGY OF NAME CHANGES

    1869 -   Straight College
    1930 -   Dillard University

LOCATION

Dillard is located in Louisiana's cultural center, the beautiful city of New Orleans, - home of the Mardi Gras - where the flavor is of a glamorous past, preserved in the Vieux Carre. All means of public transportation are available in the city. Part of the pleasant experience associated with attending Dillard is its location in New Orleans. The city is noted for its fine food and entertainment.

The Address: **Dillard University**
2601 Gentilly Boulevard
New Orleans, Louisiana 70122
Telephone: (504) 283-8822

THE INSTITUTION

The University is a private co-educational liberal arts undergraduate institution. It is located on a forty-six-acre tract in a lovely residential section of New Orleans. The campus consists of 19 white buildings and oak-shaded pathways and it has been called one of the prettiest colleges in the country. The enrollment is approximately 1400. Five residence halls are available and housing on campus is on a first-come first-served basis.

The academic program consists of six divisions of study, with majors in more than 30 areas including Japanese studies: The six divisions are:

- Division of Business
- Division of Education
- Division of Humanities
- Division of Natural Sciences
- Division of Nursing
- Division of Social Sciences

The Bachelor of Arts, Bachelor of Science and the Bachelor of Science in Nursing are conferred.

FEES

Cost per academic year: tuition, room and board $9000.

DISTINGUISHED ALUMNI

Dr. William W. Sutton   -   President, Mississippi Valley State University

Judge Robert F. Collins   -   U.S. District Judge Eastern Division, Louisiana

Earl Lucas   -   Mayor, Mississippi's All-Black Township Mount Bayou

GRAMBLING STATE UNIVERSITY

Grambling, founded by Charles P. Adams, was established as the Colored Industrial and Agricultural school in 1901. It became a state junior college in 1928 and a four-year college in 1940. The first baccalaureate degree was awarded in 1944.

CHRONOLOGY OF NAME CHANGES

1901	-	Colored Industrial and Agricultural School
1905	-	North Louisiana Agricultural and Industrial Institute
1918	-	Lincoln Parrish Training School
1928	-	Louisiana Normal and Industrial Institute
1947	-	Grambling College
1974	-	Grambling State University

LOCATION

Grambling is located in the northern part of Louisiana, sixty-five miles from the nearest metropolitan area, Shreveport, which is the third largest city in Louisiana. The airport is 40 miles from campus and public transportation provides easy access to the campus.

The Address: **Grambling State University**
Post Office Box 605
Grambling, Louisiana 71245
Telephone: (318) 247-3811

THE INSTITUTION

The university is a public-supported co-educational institution with an enrollment of 7000 students. There are fifty-six buildings on 240 acres. Residence halls house 67 percent of the students. The student/faculty ratio is twenty-to-one. The degree granting academic units are Colleges of Liberal Arts, Science and Technology,

Education, and the School of Nursing, Social Work and the Graduate Division. The baccalaureate degree is offered in biological science, business administration, communications, computer and information sciences, education, engineering, fine and applied arts, health professions, mathematics, physical sciences, psychology, public affairs and service, and social sciences. The master's degree is conferred in liberal studies, education, business administration, social work, criminal justice, and public administration. The doctoral degree is offered in Developmental Education.

A dual-degree program in engineering and cross-registration is offered with Louisiana Technical University. Study abroad is available in Mexico and South America.

FEES

Cost per academic year: tuition $3500, room and board $3000.

DISTINGUISHED ALUMNI

Joseph B. Johnson	-	President of Talladega
Judy Ann Mason	-	Television Script Writer
Willie Davis	-	Professional Football Player Green Bay Packers
Doug Williams	-	Professional Football Player Washington Redskins
James Harris	-	Professional Football Player Los Angeles Rams

SOUTHERN UNIVERSITY

Southern University is more than a single university. It is a system. Following along the Red River from Shreveport to Baton Rouge to New Orleans are the institutions that are part of the System. The Southern University System is the only predominantly Black public university System in the nation. With its three major campuses, it covers a total campus area of 1000 acres and has more than 20,000 students.

The Baton Rouge campus was the first of the System institutions to be established. It is the oldest and the largest and the only one that offers post-baccalaureate degrees. Baton Rouge, the capital city of Louisiana, a characterized by winding drives, scenic lakes, bayous and ante-bellum homes. With this setting as a surrounding, the campus presents a very impressive environment. The campus was chartered as Southern University in New Orleans in 1880. The name, Baton Rouge, was adopted in 1890 when the college moved and became a land-grant institution in 1892.

The New Orleans campus is primarily a commuter campus serving the greater New Orleans area. It has no dormitories.

Shreveport, the two-year campus, located in the northeast corner of the state, is a part of the third largest city in Louisiana.

 The Law School is located on the Baton Rouge campus and has an administration separate from the Baton Rouge Campus. It is the newest member of the System.

LOCATION

System Office is located in Baton Rouge: **(504) 771-4680**

The members of the System are:

Southern University - New Orleans
6400 Press Drive
New Orleans, Louisiana 70126
Telephone: (504) 286-5000

Southern University - Baton Rouge
P.O. Box 9614
Southern Branch Post Office
Baton Rouge, Louisiana 70813
Telephone: (504) 711-5020

Southern University Law Center (SULA)
Lenoir Hall
Baton Rouge, Louisiana 70813
Telephone: (504) 771-5020

Southern University - Shreveport
MLK Drive
Shreveport, Louisiana 71107
Telephone (318) 674-3300

THE INSTITUTION

Spread out in a relatively straight line from Shreveport to New Orleans, the Southern University System provides most of the options for academic majors available in a large institution.
If one is interested in attending one of the system institutions, write directly to the campus of your choice for information.

With the exception of the Law School, all of the campuses offer the baccalaureate degree in accounting, art, biology, business administration, chemistry, computer science, physics, psychology, sociology and speech.

Unique to a particular campus are the following:

- Baton Rouge campus—agriculture, architecture, drama, geography, microbiology, music, and nursing.

- New Orleans campus - medical technology and zoology.

FEES

Cost per academic year: tuition, room and board $6000.

DISTINGUISHED ALUMNI

Dolores R. Spiles	-	President, Southern Univ. System
Willie Davenport	-	1968 Olympic Gold-Medalist
Clarence Williams	-	Performing Artist
Norward J. Brooks	-	Seattle City Comptroller
William J. Jefferson	-	Louisiana's first Black Congressman

XAVIER UNIVERSITY

Xavier University is the only Black Roman Catholic University in the South. The Sisters of the Blessed Sacrament with Katharine Drexel founded the school in 1925 to provide an affordable college education to Black and Indian Catholic youth.

CHRONOLOGY

1915	-	Established as a secondary school
1918	-	Chartered
1925	-	Became a 4-year college
1928	-	Awarded first baccalaureate degree
1933	-	Added the master's program

LOCATION

The twenty-seven-acre campus is located only minutes from the heart of New Orleans. It is served by the mass transit system, an airport eight miles from campus and passenger rail less than two miles from campus.

The Address: **Xavier University**
7325 Palmetto and Pine Streets
New Orleans, Louisiana 70125
Telephone: (504) 486-7411

THE INSTITUTION

Xavier is a private co-educational institution with an average enrollment of 2500. On-campus residence halls house 25 percent of the student body. The student/faculty ratio is fifteen-to-one.

Xavier is credited with educating 15 percent of all African-American pharmacists in the nation. The campus is ruled by the natural sciences, the area in which over 50 percent of its students major. Additionally, the university awards the baccalaureate in accounting, chemistry, communication, computer science, economics, education, engineering, English, health and physical education, history, marketing, mathematics, microbiology, music, pharmacology, philosophy, physics, political science, psychology, social science, speech pathology, statistics, and theology.

FEES

Cost per academic year: tuition $5000, room and board $3000.

DISTINGUISHED ALUMNI

George McKenna	-	Superintendent of Schools Inglewood, California
Alexis Herman	-	Democratic National Committee Chief-of-Staff; Named one of the 100 top outstanding business women in the U.S.
Norman C. Francis	-	Alumnus President of Xavier
Brenda August	-	Decennial Specialist U.S. Dept. of Commerce
Andolyn V. Brown	-	Vice President, Student Affairs, Wilberforce University

 *Maryland*

5 H/PBCUs

BOWIE STATE COLLEGE

Bowie was originally established as an Industrial School for Colored Youth in 1865. The first instruction at the postsecondary level was offered in 1893; the first baccalaureate degree was awarded in 1912.

CHRONOLOGY OF NAME CHANGES

1865	-	Industrial School for Colored Youth
1908	-	Normal School No. 3
1912	-	Bowie Normal and Industrial School
1925	-	Maryland State Teachers College
1963	-	Bowie State College

LOCATION

The location of Bowie State is described as being "at the center of a triangle" formed by the nation's capital (Washington, D.C.), Annapolis, and Baltimore, MD. The university is situated in the suburbs, the natural boundary of trees and forests gives the university a country-like setting.

The Washington Metropolitan Area Transit Authority (METRO), a passenger rail system and air transportation is available to serve the Bowie campus.

The Address: **Bowie State College**
Jericho Park Road
Bowie, Maryland 20715
Telephone: (301) 464-6563

THE INSTITUTION

The campus has a total of 17 buildings on 237 acres. Tremendous growth occurred during the 1970s with the construction of the Communication Arts Center, the administration building, the physical education complex, a new library and a six-story residence hall.

Students can select from twenty-seven major fields of study. These majors, grouped by department, are:

- Behavioral Sciences and Human Services
- Business, Economics, Public Administration
- Communications
- Education and Physical Education
- History, Politics, and International Studies
- Humanities and Fine Arts
- Natural Sciences, Mathematics, and Computer Science
- Nursing
- Military Science

These departments are divided into four major area:

- Humanities
- Social Science
- Mathematics/Science
- Education/Physical Ed.

The university offers dual programs in dentistry and engineering with the University of Maryland.

Two undergraduate degrees are awarded: Bachelor of Science and Bachelor of Arts. Bowie State is a NCAA Division II school. Students may participate in many types of sports: football, women's volleyball, men's and women's basketball, co-educational track and field softball, baseball, and co-educational tennis. The school offers sports scholarships.

In addition to the opportunities to participate in team sports, at Bowie more than 40 different activities are available for the students. These include sororities and fraternities, academic clubs, pre-professional organizations, musical organizations and drama clubs to list a few. With an average enrollment of 3000 students, eighty-five percent are from Maryland, the remaining 15 percent from several other states and 40 foreign countries.

On-campus housing is available for 600 students. The residence halls-Harriet Tubman, Lucretia Kennard, Dwight Holmes and the Towers, are situated on the south end of the campus. A new Honors Residence Hall houses 30 students. The university has a multicultural, multi-racial faculty, 60 percent of whom hold the doctoral degree. The student/faculty ratio is fifteen-to-one.

FEES

Cost per academic year: tuition, room and board $7000.

DISTINGUISHED ALUMNI

Lula M. Loynes	-	Subcontracts Administrator
		Lockheed Engr. & Mgnt. Services
John A. Austin	-	Professor, Norfolk State Univ.
Kevin L. Jefferson	-	National Minority Affairs
		Coordinator for Handgun Control

COPPIN STATE COLLEGE

The college was named for Fanny Jackson Coppin, who was born a slave in the District of Columbia in 1837. She was one of the first Black women to earn a degree from a major U.S. college. Coppin State College was established as a postsecondary institution offering teacher training in 1900. Initially housed in Douglass High School, it became a four-year college in 1930. The first baccalaureate degree was awarded in 1942 and in 1950 it became part of the Maryland Educational System.

CHRONOLOGY OF NAME CHANGES

1900	-	Douglass High School
1926	-	Fannie Jackson Coppin Normal School
1930	-	Coppin Teachers College
1950	-	Copin State Teachers College
1967	-	Coppin State College

LOCATION

Coppin is very much a part of Baltimore, the largest city in Maryland. The tree-lined campus occupies 38 acres in west Baltimore and is one of the city's most impressive settings for learning. It is an urban campus with easy access to public transportation. The Metro stops at Mondawin Mall, a five minute walk from campus. The proximity to the national capital makes Baltimore a city with rich heritage. Just outside the city, on a point reaching into the harbor, is the site of major bombardment during the War of 1812, which inspired Francis Scott Key to write the "Star Spangled Banner".

The Address: **Coppin State College**
2500 West North Avenue
Baltimore, Maryland 21216
Telephone: (301) 333-5990

THE INSTITUTION

Enrollment varies but generally services 2300 to 3000 students. The majority of the students are from the Baltimore/District of Columbia area. Intercollegiate athletics for men and women are available. There is no on-campus housing. The student/faculty ratio is fifteen-to-one. There are more than 40 clubs and organizations available for student participation.

Dual-degree options are available with the Maryland State Colleges; including engineering, chemistry, general science, pre-dental, pre-pharmacy, and theology with University of Maryland. The college is divided into three major undergraduate divisions. These are:
- Division of Arts and Science
- Division of Nursing
- Division of Education

The Graduate program awards degrees in the following:
- Adult and Continuing Education
- Criminal Justice
- Correctional Education
- Rehabilitation Counseling
- Special Education

FEES

Cost per academic year: tuition $4000.

DISTINGUISHED ALUMNI

Milton Burk Allen   -   Chief Prosecutor, Maryland State Attorney for Baltimore

MORGAN STATE UNIVERSITY

Morgan State University was chartered as Centenary Bible Institution and offered first instruction at postsecondary level in 1867. The first baccalaureate degree was offered in 1895.

CHRONOLOGY OF NAME CHANGES

1867 - Centenary Bible Institute
1890 - Morgan College
1939 - Morgan State College
1975 - Morgan State University

LOCATION

Located in the northeast section of Baltimore, Maryland's largest city, students have access to a mass transit bus system, passenger rail and airport facilities. Easily accessible by car or by public transportation, the campus enjoys a residential setting with a suburban feeling. Proximity to the national capital makes this college an interesting choice.

The Address: **Morgan State University**
Cold Spring Lane
Baltimore, Maryland 21239
Telephone: (301) 444-3300

THE INSTITUTION

Morgan is a public co-educational institution located on 130 acres with an enrollment of 4500 students. The student/faculty ratio is sixteen-to-one. Available for students is the option to participate in a variety of cooperative programs including the dual-degree in engineering with University of Pennsylvania and University of

Rochester; physical therapy with University of Maryland. Cross-registration is available with Bowie State College, College of Notre Dame, Coppin State College, Goucher College, John Hopkins University, Salisbury State College, University of Baltimore and the University of Maryland. The college is divided into four divisions:

- College of Arts and Science
- School of Business Management
- School of Education and Urban
- School of Engineering

Majors are offered in accounting, architecture, art/advertising, biology, chemistry, communications, computer science, drama/theater, ecology, education, engineering, health/physical education, home economics, human services, medical technology, military science, philosophy, physics, political science, psychology, religion, social welfare work and speech.

FEES

Cost per academic year: $3500, room and board: $3500.

DISTINGUISHED ALUMNI

Earl Graves	-	Publisher, Black Enterprise
Wilson W. Goode	-	Mayor, Philadelphia
Parren J. Mitchell	-	Former U.S. Congressman
Hilda L. Joyce	-	Asst. Professor University of Virgin Islands
Willie Lanier	-	Professional Football Player Kansas City Chiefs
Frederick Oliver Boone	-	Pilot, Delta Airlines

SOJOURNER-DOUGLASS COLLEGE

Sojourner-Douglass was founded and chartered in 1972 as an affiliate to Antioch University, Ohio. The College is a unique, community-controlled private institution offering an educational alternative for working adults. It provides an opportunity for adult learners to study on a full-time basis by providing evening and weekend classes. The name Sojourner-Douglass was selected to honor the historical contributions of two Black abolitionist–Sojourner Truth and Frederick Douglass.

LOCATION

The address: **Sojourner Douglass College**
500 North Caroline Street
Baltimore, Maryland, 21205
Telephone: (301) 276-0306

THE INSTITUTION

Sojourner is a small (average 400 students per year) college that awards the Bachelor of Arts degree. Sojourner operates on a trimester system (3 terms - 15 weeks each). A student may design a career speciality in any combination of the three major areas:

Administration:
- Administration and Management
- Public Administration
- Hospitality Management
- Business Admin.
- Health Care Admin
- Cable TV Admin.

Human and Social Resources areas:
- Criminal Justice
- Community Development
- Social Work
- Gerontology
- Social Welfare

Human Growth and Development:
- Early Childhood Education
- Psychology

FEES

Cost per academic trimester: tuition $1600.

DISTINGUISHED ALUMNI

Hattie N. Harrison	-	Member, House of Delegates, Baltimore, 1st Black woman to chair a legislative committee
Nathan C. Irby	-	Member of the Senate, Baltimore

UNIVERSITY OF MARYLAND
EASTERN SHORE

The university is a co-educational institution established in 1886.

CHRONOLOGY OF NAME CHANGES

    1886 - Princess Anne of the Delaware Conference
    1948 - Maryland State College
    1970 - University of Maryland - Eastern Shore

LOCATION

The six-hundred-acre campus is located in the southeast corner of Maryland approximately half-way between the states of Delaware and Virginia. It is a college town and the majority of the population is involved in the institution. Baltimore and D.C. are approximately 130 miles from campus.

The Address: **University of Maryland (E.S.)**
                   Princess Anne, Maryland 21853
                   Telephone: (301) 651-2200

THE INSTITUTION

The university is a co-educational institution with an enrollment of 1500. On-campus housing can accommodate fifty-five percent of the students. The student/faculty ratio is fifteen-to-one.

Degrees are offered in accounting, agriculture, airway science, allied health fields, art/advertisement, biology, building construction, business administration, chemistry, communication, computer science, counseling/student personnel, curriculum and instruction, ecology, economics, education, engineering, English, history, home economics, hotel and restaurant management, industrial arts, mathematics, music, physical education, physical therapy, and the social sciences.

FEES

Cost per academic year: tuition $4000, room: $2000, board $1500.

DISTINGUISHED ALUMNI

Ambrose Jearld, Jr.	-	Chief Research Planner
		National Marine Fisheries Service
		U.S. Department. of Commerce
Emmet H. Paige, Jr.	-	1971, Army's 1st Black General
Martin J. Lamkin	-	Music Instructor
		University of Virgin Islands

1 H/PBCU

MARYGROVE COLLEGE

Marygrove College was established in 1845 by the Servants of the Immaculate Heart of Mary Sisters (IHMS). It was originally a Catholic women's college under the leadership of Theresa Maxis, a woman of color from Haiti. The college, dedicated to assisting women in developing personal values, started with approximately 300 students. Over the years the mission of the college has changed and it is currently a co-educational liberal arts college.

CHRONOLOGY OF NAME CHANGES

1845 - St. Mary Academy
1925 - St. Mary College
1927 - Marygrove College

LOCATION

The campus is located on an eighty-acre tract in northwest Detroit - the "Motor Capital of the World". There is excellent transportation by bus, passenger rail and air.

The Address: **Marygrove College**
                  8425 W. McNichols Road
                  Detroit, Michigan 48221
                  Telephone: (313) 862-8000

THE INSTITUTION

Marygrove College is an independent Catholic liberal arts college. The metropolitan campus offers dormitory accommodations for 50 percent of the approximate 1200 students on a first-come first-served basis. The degrees offered include the baccalaureate and the master's as well as the Associate in Arts and the Associate in Science. Degree programs are offered in accounting, allied health, arts, biology, business, chemistry, child development, communications, computer science, correctional science, dance, English, fashion merchandising, history, human ecology, mathematics, music, performing arts, physical science, psychology, and religion. The school curriculum also includes courses leading to pre-medicine and pre-law degrees.

The first-year seminar is an introduction to college life and assists students in developing academic and personal success in life. It is recommended for all beginning students.

FEES

Cost per academic semester: tuition $3300, private room and board $2000.

Mississippi

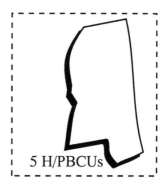

5 H/PBCUs

ALCORN STATE UNIVERSITY

Alcorn State University was established in 1871 on the site of a closed Presbyterian school for boys. It is the oldest predominantly Black land-grant institution in the United States. Located on the campus is the Oakland Memorial Chapel recognized as a nationally historic site and the location of the conferring of the first degree in the state of Mississippi.

CHRONOLOGY OF NAME CHANGES

1871	-	Alcorn University
1878	-	Alcorn Agriculture and Mechanical College
1974	-	Alcorn State University

LOCATION

Alcorn is equidistant from Vicksburg to the north and Natchez to the south, and 80 miles from Jackson. It is served by an airport 35 miles from campus and by passenger rail 90 miles away. The campus is situated in Lorman, Mississippi; surrounded with the ruins of beautiful Windsor Castle and the gigantic Mississippi river. These sites blend well with the school's century-old buildings and moss-draped trees, together creating a beautiful historic setting.

The Address: **Alcorn State University**
                 P.O. Box 300
                 Lorman, Mississippi 39096
                 Telephone: (601) 877-2691

THE INSTITUTION

Alcorn is a co-educational college with an enrollment about 3000 and a student/faculty ratio of fifteen-to-one. Most of the students live on campus in beautiful modern air-conditioned dormitories. The campus is composed of 105 buildings some of which have been designated national monuments.

The University awards the Bachelor of Science, Bachelor of Arts and the Bachelor of Music through the following divisions:
- Division of Arts and Sciences
- Division of Education and Psychology
- Division of Agriculture and Applied Science
- Division of Business and Economics
- Division of Nursing
- Division of General College for Excellence

The Division of Graduate Studies awards the Master of Science in Education and Master of Science in Agriculture.

FEES

Cost per academic semester: tuition, room and board $3000.

DISTINGUISHED ALUMNI

Del Anderson   -   President, San Jose City College (CA)
Alex Haley   -   Author of Roots

JACKSON STATE UNIVERSITY

Established by American Baptist Home Mission Society in 1877, the school was designed to provide training for Black youth. It is the fourth largest state-supported university in Mississippi. The first instruction at the postsecondary level was offered in 1921, and the first baccalaureate degree was awarded in 1924.

CHRONOLOGY OF NAME CHANGES

1877	-	Natchez Seminary
1940	-	Mississippi Negro Training School
1944	-	Jackson College for Negro Teachers
1956	-	Jackson State College
1974	-	Jackson State University

LOCATION

The college is located in Jackson, the capital and largest metropolitan area in Mississippi. Transportation to and from the campus is available by mass transit bus system. An airport is eight miles away and passenger rail service is two miles from campus.

The Address: **Jackson State University**
1400 John R. Lynch Street
Jackson, Mississippi 39217
Telephone: (601) 968-2121

THE INSTITUTION

Jackson is a state-supported institution with an average enrollment of 6500. On-campus housing is provided for thirty-two percent of the student body. The ratio of students to faculty is twenty-one-to-one. The bachelor's, master's and doctorate degrees are awarded for those who successfully complete prescribed curricula. The academic program is provided through four schools:

- The School of Liberal Studies
- The School of Business
- The School of Education
- The School of Science and Technology

The programs available are accounting, art biology, business administration, communication, computer science, criminal justice, ecology, economics, education, English, guidance, health and physical education, industrial administration, industrial arts, management, mathematics, music, physics, political science, psychology, reading education, social science, sociology, speech and urban affairs.

FEES

Cost per academic year: tuition $3000, room $1500, board $1,200.

DISTINGUISHED ALUMNI

J. Paul Brownridge   -   City Treasure, Los Angeles
Walter Payton   -   Pro-football player
                         Chicago Bears
Mary L. Smith   -   Interim President
                         Kentucky State University
Gladys J. Willis   -   Chairperson, English Dept.
                         Lincoln University (PA)
Robert G. Clark   -   Politician, Representative,
                         State of Mississippi
                         District 47

MISSISSIPPI VALLEY STATE UNIVERSITY

The University was created by an Act of the Mississippi State Legislature in 1946. It was opened for service to students in the summer of 1950. The first baccalaureate degrees were awarded in 1953 to its first graduating class of 13.

CHRONOLOGY OF NAME CHANGES

1946 - Mississippi Vocational College
1964 - Mississippi Valley State College
1974 - Mississippi Valley State University

LOCATION

Mississippi Valley is located in the small town of Itta Bena less than 90 miles north of Jackson and about 50 miles from the Arkansas border and the great Mississippi River.

The Address: **Mississippi Valley State University**
Itta Bena, Mississippi 38941
Telephone: (601) 254-9041

THE INSTITUTION

The university has nine departments offering 700 different courses annually and awarding degrees in 30 areas. Students may select majors in the following areas: art/advertisement, biology, business administration, computer science, mathematics, music, education, health, physical education and recreation, industrial technology, social work, speech, environmental health, criminal justice, political/ science and government, office administration, sociology, English and visual and performing arts.

Additionally, a cooperative program in oceanography with the Gulf Coast Research Laboratory is available. The average enrollment is approximately 2000 and the student/faculty ratio is eighteen-to-one. The university awards the Bachelor of Arts, Bachelor of Science, Bachelor of Music, Master of Science in Environmental Health and Master of Science in Elementary Education.

There are accommodations available for a total of 1914 students in 11 dormitory units. Space is allocated on a first-come first-served basis.

FEES

Cost per academic year: tuition $4700.

DISTINGUISHED ALUMNI

| Fannye E. Love | - | Chairperson, Teacher Education LeMoyne-Owen College |
| Hampton Smith | - | Professor, Health and Physical Education, Albany State College |

RUST COLLEGE

Rust College was founded by the Freedman's Aid Society of the Methodist Episcopal Church at a time when the South had been devastated by the Civil War. Groups such as the Freedman's Aid Society set about providing an education for the newly freed slaves. More than 4000 such schools were established, most failed. Rust survived. It is the oldest historically Black college in the state.

CHRONOLOGY OF NAME CHANGES

1866	-	Shaw School
1870	-	Shaw University
1915	-	Rust College

LOCATION

The college is located in the north-central part of the state of Mississippi. It is ten miles from the Tennessee border on the north, 50 miles from the Arkansas border on the west and approximately forty-five miles southeast of Memphis, the nearest metropoitan city.

The Address:	**Rust College**
Holly Springs, Mississippi 38635
Telephone: (601) 252-4661

THE INSTITUTION

Rust College is a co-educational liberal arts institution affiliated with the United Methodist Church. It has an average enrollment of 800 and housing facilities to accommodate approximately 90 percent of the students The student/faculty ratio is twenty-to-one. The campus covers 125 acres and has available thirty-four buildings.

The college awards the Bachelor of Arts degree in 20 majors. Course offerings are organized under five divisions: a sixth division, Freshman Studies, is an interdisciplinary program designed to aid the student in acclimation to college work.

The divisions:
- Business
- Social Sciences
- Education
- Humanities
- Science and Mathematics

Dual-degree programs are available: in engineering with Georgia Institute of Technology, Memphis State University, Tuskegee University and University of Mississippi; in health careers with Meharry Medical School; and in nursing with Alcorn State University.

FEES

Cost per academic year: tuition $3500, room and board $2000.

DISTINGUISHED ALUMNI

David L. Beckley - President, Wiley College
Lonear Heard - Owner, McDonald Franchise
Ida L. Jackson - First Black teacher, Oakland, CA Public Schools and Eighth Supreme Basileus AKA Sorority
Ida B. Wells - An organizer of the NAACP

TOUGALOO COLLEGE

Tougaloo College was founded in 1869 by the American Missionary Society of New York. It is today a private college affiliated with the United Church of Christ and the Christian Church (Disciples of Christ). It offered the first postsecondary level in 1897 and the first baccalaureate degree was awarded in 1901.

CHRONOLOGY OF NAME CHANGES

1869	-	Tougaloo College
1871	-	Tougaloo University
1916	-	Tougaloo College
1954	-	Tougaloo Christian College
1963	-	Tougaloo College

LOCATION

The college is located in the Jackson metropolitan area. Jackson is the state capital and the largest city in the state. There is available a mass transit bus system and an airport less than 200 miles from campus.

The Address: **Tougaloo College**
Tougaloo, Mississippi 39174
Telephone: (601) 956-4941

THE INSTITUTION

The five-hundred-and-nine-acre campus has 14 major buildings and a student enrollment that averages 800. On-campus residence halls house 70 percent of the student body. The college offers dual-degree programs, student exchange programs and/or cross-registration with several colleges. This would include Brown

University, Georgia Institute of Technology, Howard University, Tuskegee University, University of Mississippi, University of Wisconsin-Madison, Bowdoin College, Meharry Medical College and Millsaps College.

Degrees are offered in accounting, art/advertising, biology, business, chemistry, communications, computer science, economics, education, engineering, English, gerontology, history, humanities, journalism, mathematics, music, physical education, physics, political science, psychology, social welfare, and sociology.

FEES

Cost per academic year: tuition $3500, room and board $2000.

DISTINGUISHED ALUMNI

Dr. Walter Washington	-	President, Alcorn State University
Dr. Oscar A. Rogers, Jr.	-	President, Claflin College
Elaine Baker	-	Professor, Albany State
Terrecia W. Sweet	-	Professor, California State University, Fresno

Missouri

2 H/PBCUs

HARRIS-STOWE STATE COLLEGE

Harris-Stowe State College was founded in 1857 by the St. Louis Public Schools as a Normal school. It was the first public teacher education institution west of the Mississippi River and the twelfth such institution in the United States. Harris-Stowe had two predecessor institutions: The Normal school was originally established for white students only; Stowe Teachers' College, which began in1890, was the Normal school for Black future teachers. The two teacher education institutions were merged by the Board of Education of the St. Louis Public Schools in 1954. This was the first of several steps to integrate the pubic schools of St. Louis.

CHRONOLOGY OF NAME CHANGES

1857	-	Harris Teachers College
1890	-	Stowe Teachers College
1924	-	The Sumner Normal School
1929	-	Stowe Teachers College
1954	-	Harris Teachers College
1979	-	Harris-Stowe State College

LOCATION

The college is located at the hub of metropolitan St. Louis with access to Interstate Highways 44 and 55 and U.S. Highway 40. It is easily reached by public transportation facilities.

The Address: **Harris-Stowe State College**
                 3026 - LaClede Avenue
                 St. Louis, Missouri 63103
                 Telephone: (314) 533-3000

THE INSTITUTION

This is a public co-educational institution, with an average enrollment of 1400 students. In 1981, the college received state approval for the Bachelor of Science in Urban Education. This program was at that time the only one of its kind at the undergraduate level in the United States. The programs at Harris-Stowe are devoted exclusively to professional education development, which covers three main fields: teacher development, urban education specialist development and career enrichment. The disciplines addressed at Harris-Stowe are: accounting, aerospace, anthropology/sociology, art, biology, business administration, chemistry, computer science, dance, economics, education, English, French, geography, history, industrial arts, journalism, mathematics, meteorology, philosophy, physical education, physical science, physics, Spanish, speech, theater and urban education.

FEES

Cost per academic year: tuition $5000.

DISTINGUISHED ALUMNI

George Hyran -   Vice President, Emeritus Harris-Stowe

LINCOLN UNIVERSITY (MO)

The University was founded by a white officer and a Black enlisted man who fought for the Union during the Civil war. It was established as a private school in 1866 and became a state institute in 1879. The first instruction at the postsecondary level was offered in 1877 and the first baccalaureate degree was awarded in 1891.

CHRONOLOGY OF NAME CHANGES

1866 - Lincoln Institute
1921 - Lincoln University

LOCATION

Lincoln University is located in the capital city of Missouri, Jefferson City. Students attending this university have available all of the benefits of a capital city. Mass transit bus system, an airport twenty-five miles from campus and passenger rail service approximately one mile from campus provide easy access to the campus.

The Address: **Lincoln University**
820 Chestnut Street
Jefferson City, Missouri 65101
Telephone: (314) 681-5000 and 681-5024

THE INSTITUTION

The university is a comprehensive, multipurpose campus offering the associate, baccalaureate, and the master's degrees in 55 degree programs: 44 undergraduate and 11 graduate.

In addition to the main campus of 136 acres, the university has a research farm that encompasses more than 800 acres. The public co-educational school has an average enrollment of 2500 students and on-campus housing can accommodate 50 percent of the student body. The student/faculty ratio is twenty-to-one. The areas of academic concentration are agriculture, business/economics, education, English, fine arts, foreign language, health/physical education, home economics, journalism, natural sciences, nursing science, philosophy, psychology, and social sciences.

FEES

Cost per academic year: tuition $2600, room $1500, board $2000.

DISTINGUISHED ALUMNI

Roland Copes	-	Vice President, Human Resources Division, Massachusetts Mutual Life Insurance Company
Dr. Henry Givens, Jr.	-	President, Harris-Stowe State College

New Jersey

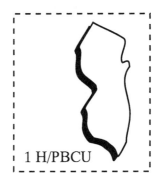

1 H/PBCU

BLOOMFIELD COLLEGE

Bloomfield College was established in the mid 1800s as a training school for German speaking ministers. Today, it is a liberal arts college affiliated with the Presbyterian church.

CHRONOLOGY OF NAME CHANGES

    1913 -   Bloomfield Theological Seminary
    1926 -   Bloomfield College

LOCATION

Bloomfield is located in the northern section of the state of New Jersey. It is approximately ten miles northwest of Newark and 25 miles west of New York City. Transportation to and from the campus is provided by bus, train and air. Bus service from the campus to the airport and/or the train station is readily available. Proximity to New York makes this a very exciting campus.

The Address: **Bloomfield College**
                Bloomfield, New Jersey 07003
                Telephone: (201) 748-9000

THE INSTITUTION

The 1200 student-body campus offers the Bachelor of Arts degree in economics, English, fine and performing arts, French, history, inter-disciplinary studies, philosophy, religion, sociology and Spanish. The Bachelor of Science degree is available in accounting, biology, business administration, chemistry and nursing.

On-campus living is available in dormitories and the Honors house. The school also operates several off-campus apartments to accommodate students. Priority for on-campus housing is given to freshmen.

FEES

Cost per academic year: tuition $7400, room and board $3800.

DISTINGUISHED ALUMNI

Juan Simpson	-	New Products Controller, Johnson & Johnson, Piscataway, N.J.
Manuel Suarez	-	Professor of Modern Language University of the Virgin Islands

2 H/PBCU's

COLLEGE FOR HUMAN SERVICES

In 1964, Audrey C. Cohen founded the College for Human Services and the college was charted in 1970. It was described as a new kind of educational institution. At the College for Human Services emphasis was turned from an economy based on manufacturing toward an economy based on service. The mission of the college is to provide the kind of education needed for service-oriented corporations and businesses. In 1984 the college received full accreditation as a pioneer in education for the new economy. The college was started with less than 300 students. Current enrollment averages 1200.

The Address: **College for Human Services**
                345 Hudson Street
                New York, New York 10014
                Telephone: (212) 989-2002

THE INSTITUTION

The college offers a performance-based baccalaureate program. With a major emphasis in human service, the baccalaureate degree is awarded in business administration, business education and human services. This is primarily a commuter school.

There are no dormitories.

FEES

Cost per academic semester: tuition $4000.

MEDGAR EVERS COLLEGE (CUNY)

Medgar Evers College, founded in 1969 as a result of community efforts, is named in memory of the slain civil rights leader. The College was established to meet the educational needs of the Central Brooklyn community from which it draws 85 percent of its students. The student population is 92 percent Black, and includes people with roots in seventy-five countries including the Caribbean and Africa. Approximately 71 percent of the student population is female and more than 50 percent of the student population is 25 years or older. The College's mission is to provide high quality, professional, career-oriented undergraduate degree programs within the context of a liberal arts curriculum, through the offering of both associates and baccalaureate degrees.

LOCATION

Situated in Central Brooklyn, access to Medgar Evers College is readily available. The multifaceted nature of New York City's mass transit system (bus, subway and taxis) minimize the necessity to have a car. The multi-cultural diversification of the neighborhood in which Medgar Evers is located, compliments the diversity in the classroom as well as the environment surrounding the institution.

The Address: **Medgar Evers College (CUNY)**
1650 Bedford Avenue
Brooklyn, New York 11225
Telephone: (718) 270-4900 or 270-6000

THE INSTITUTION

The co-educational institution is one of 17 colleges within the City University of New York System. A broad range of course offerings is available as major areas of concentration. The college offers 8 baccalaureate degree programs in accounting, business administration, nursing, public administration, biology, elementary education, special education, and psychology. Associate degree programs are offered in the following areas: secretarial science, computer applications, business administration, liberal arts (humanities and social sciences), nursing science, public administration, and elementary education. Soon to be added to the baccalaureate degree offerings will be the bachelor's degree in mathematics and environmental science.

The College has a number of special Centers and programs designed to assist students in the successful completion of their academic endeavors including: The Center for Law and Social Justice, The Caribbean Research Center, The Center for Women's Development, The Center for the Study and Resolution of Black and Latino Male Initiatives, the Jackie Robinson Center for Physical Culture and the Ralph Bunche Center for Public Policy.

Enrollment averages 4000 students, however, there are no on-campus housing facilities.

FEES

Cost per academic semester: tuition $900.

DISTINGUISHED ALUMNI/STAFF

Dr. Betty Shabazz - Wife of Malcolm Shabazz (Malcolm X)
A member of the College staff.

 *North Carolina*

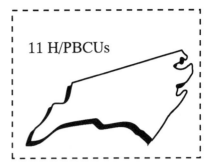

11 H/PBCUs

BARBER-SCOTIA COLLEGE

Founded in 1867 by Reverend Luke Dorland, Barber-Scotia College is a four-year independent co-educational institution affiliated with the Presbyterian Church. The original mission of the college was to train young Negro women as teachers and as social workers. In 1930, Barber Memorial merged with Soctia Women's College and in 1954, the College became co-educational.

CHRONOLOGY OF NAME CHANGES

    1867 -   Scotia Seminary
    1916 -   Scotia Women's College
    1932 -   Barber-Scotia College

LOCATION

Barber-Scotia is located in Concord, North Carolina, a city of approximately 30,000. It is served by Southern Railway; Charlotte-Douglas International Airport is only 30 miles away.

The Address: **Barber-Scotia College**
145 Cabarrus Avenue
Concord, North Carolina 28025
Telephone: (704) 786-5171

THE INSTITUTION

Twenty-five buildings are nestled on the forty-acre campus together with tennis courts, athletic and recreational areas. The small college, with nearly 600 students, provides comfortable and modern on-campus housing for ninety-five percent of the student body The students come from 15 or more states, as well as the District of Columbia, the U.S. Virgin Islands, Africa and other countries. Over 50 percent of the faculty at Barber-Scotia have received doctoral degrees and the students enjoy a student/faculty ratio of ten-to-one.

The college offers the Bachelor of Science and the Bachelor of Arts degrees. Majors are available in: accounting, biology, business administration, computer science, education, health and physical education, hotel and restaurant management, mathematics, medical technology, recreation administration and sociology.

FEES

Cost per academic year: tuition, room and board $7000; off-campus $4000.

DISTINGUISHED ALUMNI

Mary McLeod Bethune	-	Founder, President National Council of Negro Women
Eula Saxon Dean Ph.D.	-	Dean, Cosumnes River College
Mable Parker McLean	-	Former President Barber-Scotia College

BENNETT COLLEGE

Established in 1873 as a co-educational institution, the Freedman's Aid and Southern Education Society of the Methodist Episcopal Church assumed the initial responsibility for the support of the school. Chartered as a college in 1889 and reorganized as a college for women in 1926, Bennett is a private college affiliated with the United Methodist Church. It was one of the first Black colleges to be admitted into full membership in the Southern Association of Colleges and Secondary Schools.

CHRONOLOGY OF NAME CHANGES

    1873 - Bennett Seminary
    1889 - Bennett College

LOCATION

The campus is located approximately 65 miles west of Raleigh, the state capital. It is 30 miles from the Virginia border, situated in the north-central section of North Carolina. The municipal bus system and a passenger rail service is available to the campus.

The Address: **Bennett College**
                 900 East Washington Street
                 Greensboro, North Carolina 27401-3239
                 Telephone: (919) 370-8624
                 Toll-free: 1-800-338-Benn

THE INSTITUTION

The average enrollment is 600 students and forty-six percent of the students are from North Carolina, while others are from throughout the United Stated and six foreign countries. Located on the fifty-five-acre campus are twenty-four buildings, including seven residence halls with professional and peer staff. The average class has 20 students and there is a student/faculty ratio of eleven-to-one.

The Liberal Arts college has four major divisions: Education, Humanities, Social Science, and Natural Sciences. The bachelor's degree is offered in accounting, biology, business administration, chemistry, computer science, English, home economics, mathematics, political science, psychology and the health professions including nursing. Dual-degree and/or cooperative education programs are available with the following institutions:

- North Carolina Agricultural and Technical State University
- University of North Carolina - Chapel Hill
- Bowman Gray School of Medicine
- Howard University Hospital

FEES

Cost per academic year: tuition, room and board $7500.

DISTINGUISHED ALUMNI

Carolyn Robertson Payton   - 1st Female Director of the U.S. Peace Corp.

Dorothy Lavinia Brown   - 1st African-American Female Surgeon in the South

Rev. Jacquelyn Grant   - Professor, Interdenominational Theological Center

Celestine Wilson Goodloe   - Assoc. Director of Admission Xavier (OH)

ELIZABETH CITY STATE UNIVERSITY

Established as Elizabeth State Colored Normal School in 1891, the university offered the first instruction at the postsecondary level in 1937. The first baccalaureate degree was awarded in 1939.

CHRONOLOGY OF NAME CHANGES

1891	-	Elizabeth State Colored Normal School
1939	-	Elizabeth City State Teachers College
1963	-	Elizabeth City State College
1969	-	Elizabeth City State University

LOCATION

The campus of 160 acres is located in the far northeast corner of the state of North Carolina and less than 50 miles from Norfolk, Virginia. There is access to water ways that lead to the Albemarie Sound. The city is served by an airport 50 miles away as well as rail and bus service.

The Address: **Elizabeth City State University**
Parkview Drive
Elizabeth City, North Carolina 27909
Telephone: (919) 335-3400 and 335-3305

THE INSTITUTION

Elizabeth City State is a public co-educational institution. The available housing will accommodate 50 percent of the average enrollment of 1500 students. The baccalaureate degree is awarded in a number of majors including art, biological sciences, broadcasting, business and management, chemistry, computer and information sciences, criminal justice, education, English, fine and applied arts, mathematics, music, physical sciences, psychology, public affairs and social sciences. The option is also available to participate in joint programs with the Norfolk State University and North Carolina State University. The campus enjoys a twelve-to-one student/ faculty ratio.

FEES

Cost per academic year: tuition, room and board $9000.

DISTINGUISHED ALUMNI

    Dr. Jimmy R. Jenkins -   1st Alumnus to become Chancellor
                               of Elizabeth City State University
    Dr. Curtis E. Bryan   -   President, Denmark Technical
                               College (S.C.)
    Dr. Leonard Slade, Jr. -   Dean, College of Arts & Science
                               Kentucky State College

FAYETTEVILLE STATE UNIVERSITY

The University, originally established as Howard School in 1867, and designed to serve Colored people. It offered the first instruction at the postsecondary level in 1921and is now a part of the University of North Carolina system.

CHRONOLOGY OF NAME CHANGES

1867	-	Howard School
1916	-	State Colored Normal and Industrial School
1921	-	State Normal School for the Negro Race
1926	-	State normal School
1939	-	Fayetteville State Teachers College
1963	-	Fayetteville State College
1969	-	Fayetteville State University

LOCATION

Fayetteville State is located 50 miles from Raleigh and Durham, the nearest metropolitan areas. The university is served by mass transit bus system, an airport eight miles from campus and passenger rail service four miles from campus.

The Address: **Fayetteville State University**
Murchinson Road
Fayetteville, North Carolina 28301
Telephone: (919) 486-1371
1-800-222-2594

THE INSTITUTION

The campus spreads over 156 acres between Raleigh and Durham, with a student body population of 3000 and a student/faculty ratio of nineteen-to-one. On-campus residence halls house forty-eight percent of the students. The public co-educational institution offers the associate, the baccalaureate and the master's degrees. Major areas of study include biological sciences, business and management, education, fine and applied arts, mathematics physical sciences, psychology, public affairs and service, and social sciences.

Fort Bragg-Pope Air Force Base, less than 30 miles from the main campus, is the site for Servicemembers Opportunity College. The university offers the cooperative baccalaureate program in engineering with North Carolina State University at Raleigh and in medical technology with approved hospitals. Institutionally-sponsored study abroad is available.

FEES

Cost per academic year: tuition $4800, room and board $2500.

DISTINGUISHED ALUMNI

Algeania Freeman	-	Dept. Chair, Community Health & Rehabilitation, Norfolk State
Gerald Sullivan	-	Professor, Military Science Dillard University
Jerry C. Johnson	-	Athletic Director, LeMoyne-Owen College

JOHNSON C. SMITH UNIVERSITY

Johnson C. Smith was established in 1867 as a private men's institution affiliated with the Presbyterian Church. The school was charted in1869, awarded its first baccalaureate degree in 1872 and became fully co-educational in 1941.

CHRONOLOGY OF NAME CHANGES

1867 - Biddle Memorial Institute
1876 - Biddle University
1923 - Johnson C. Smith University

LOCATION

The university is located in Charlotte (less than 20 miles from the Tennessee borderline) and enjoys the transportation options that are available in a city of nearly a million people.

The Address: **Johnson C. Smith**
100-300 Bettieford Road
Charlotte, North Carolina 28216
Telephone: (704) 378-1041 and 378-1010

THE INSTITUTION

The campus has 21 buildings located on 100 acres and approximately 1200 students in attendance. On-campus housing is available. Joint degree program in engineering with University of North Carolina and in marine biology with Duke are options available for the students. The curriculum offers majors in English, foreign language, fine arts and humanities, business administration and economics, history and political science, sociology and social work, education, health and physical education, psychology, biology, chemistry, physics, computer science and mathematics. The student/faculty ratio is fifteen-to-one.

FEES

Cost per academic year: tuition $4000, room and board $2000.

DISTINGUISHED ALUMNI

Richard C. Erwin   - U.S. District Judge, Middle
                          District, North Carolina.
                          1st African-American to win
                          statewide race for an elected
                          office.
Lucy Allen   - Director, Center for
                          Educational Technology
                          University of the Virgin Islands
Mildred Mitchell-Bateman - West Virginia's 1st Black
                          Department Head - (Dept. of
                          Mental Health)

LIVINGSTONE COLLEGE

The college was founded by African Methodist Episcopal Zion Church in 1879 and named for David Livingstone, the missionary, explorer and philanthropist. The first postsecondary level instruction was offered in 1880 and the first baccalaureate degree was awarded in 1887.

CHRONOLOGY OF NAME CHANGES

1879 - Zion Wesley Institute
1885 - Zion Wesley College
1887 - Livingstone College

LOCATION

The campus encompasses 18 buildings and is located 60 miles from Charlotte, the nearest metropolitan area. The campus is served by an airport 50 miles away.

The Address: **Livingstone College**
701 West Monroe Street
Salisbury, North Carolina 28144
Telephone: (704) 638-5502

THE INSTITUTION

The college consists of two schools: an undergraduate college of arts and science and a graduate school of theology (Hood Thelogical Seminary). The undergraduate liberal arts college has four divisions:
* Business
* Humanities
* Natural Sciences
* Social and Behavioral Sciences

Three degrees are conferred: Bachelor of Arts, Bachelor of Science and Bachelor of Social Work.

Dual-degree programs are offered in engineering with Georgia Institute of Technology and Clemson University. Professional training for the ministry leading to the Master of Divinity and the Master of Religious Education is available through Hood Theological Seminary. The enrollment averages 600 and the student/faculty ratio is ten-to-one. On-campus residence halls house seventy-six percent of the student body.

FEES

Cost per academic year: tuition, room and board $6500.

DISTINGUISHED ALUMNI

Elizabeth Koontz   -   Formerly President National Education Association and Director, Women's Bureau Dept. and Labor

Alfred Leroy Edwards   -   Deputy Assistant Secretary of Agriculture, 1963

NORTH CAROLINA AGRICULTURAL AND TECHNICAL STATE UNIVERSITY

The first instruction at the college was in Raleigh in 1890 as an annex of Shaw University. The first baccalaureate degree was awarded in 1896. The institute was moved from Raleigh to Greensboro in 1893 and became a part of the state system in 1972.

CHRONOLOGY OF NAME CHANGES

1890 - A and M College for the Colored Race
1915 - Agricultural and Technical College of North Carolina
1967 - North Carolina Agricultural and Technical State University

LOCATION

Located between Raleigh and Winston-Salem, the college is served by mass transit bus system, an airport 12 miles away and passenger rail service less than five miles from campus.

The Address: **North Carolina A & T State University**
1601 Market Street
Greensboro, North Carolina 27411
Telephone: (919) 334-7500

THE INSTITUTION

The enrollment at the campus averages 6200 students and campus housing can accommodate fifty-one percent of the student body. With a student/faculty ratio of fifteen-to-one, the students have the option to major in a variety of programs. The university consists of seven schools:

- Agriculture
- Arts and Science
- Business and Economics
- Education
- Engineering
- Nursing
- Graduate Studies

The majors available through the seven schools include accounting, agribusiness, animal science, business administration, child/family development, computer science, drama, economics, education, engineering, home economics, landscaping, music, nursing, physics, political science, psychology, sociology, social work and speech.

FEES

Cost per academic year: tuition $4200, room and board $2500.

DISTINGUISHED ALUMNI

Ronald McNair	-	NASA Astronaut and Mission Specialist
Rev. Jesse L. Jackson	-	Minister, Civil Rightrs Activist President, National Rainbow Coalition
Frances Huntly-Cooper	-	Mayor, Fitchburg, WI
Robert C. Weaver	-	First African-American U.S. government cabinet member
Ann Watts McKinney	-	Dean, Graduate Studies Norfolk State University
Thomas Alex Farringon	-	President, Input Output Computer Services (MA)
Dr. Willie C. Robinson	-	President Florida Memorial College

NORTH CAROLINA CENTRAL UNIVERSITY

Originally chartered as a private religious training school, the university was changed to a state institution in 1923. The first instruction at the postsecondary level was in 1910 and the first baccalaureate was awarded in 1929. The university became a part of University of North Carolina System in 1972.

CHRONOLOGY OF NAME CHANGES

1909	-	National Religious Training School and Chatauga
1915	-	National Training School
1923	-	Durham State Normal School
1925	-	North Carolina College for Negroes
1947	-	North Carolina College at Durham
1969	-	North Carolina Central University

LOCATION

The university is located in the Raleigh-Durham metropolitan area and is served by a mass transit system as well as an airport and passenger rail service within 20 miles of the campus.

The Address: **North Carolina Central University**
1801 Fayetteville Street
Durham, North Carolina 27707
Telephone: (919) 560-6100

THE INSTITUTION

On-campus living is available for thirty-eight percent of the average enrollment of 4500 students. Housing is also available for married students on a first-come first-served basis. The campus area with 60 buildings covers 72 of the total 101 acres. The degrees awarded are bachelor's, first professional (law) and master's. The student/ faculty ratio is twenty-to-one.

Degrees are awarded in the following areas: accounting, art/ advertising, business administration, chemistry, computer sciences, counseling/student personnel, criminal justice, drama, economics, education, English, fine arts, food science and technology, foreign language, geography, health and physical education, history, home economics, library science, mathematics, music, nursing, philosophy, physics, political science and government, pre-medicine, psychology, public administration, social studies, and speech correction.

Also available is the option to participate in dual-degree programs with Georgia Institute of Technology.

FEES

Cost per academic year: tuition $4500, room and board $3000.

DISTINGUISHED ALUMNI

Daniel T. Blue, Jr.	-	Speaker of the House, State of North Carolina
Carolyn G. Morris	-	Deputy Asst. Director the FBI's highest ranking woman 1986
Dr. S. Dallas Simmons	-	9th President, Virginia Union University
Dr. Cleon Thompson, Jr.	-	Chancellor, Winston-Salem State University
Dr. B. Marshall Henderson	-	Chairperson, Biology Dept. Lincoln University (PA)
Robert Massey	-	Professional Football Player

SAINT AUGUSTINE'S COLLEGE

Saint Augustine's was established in 1867 as a private college affiliated with the Episcopal Church. The first postsecondary level instructions were offered in 1919. The school became a four-year institute in 1927 and the first baccalaureate was awarded in 1931.

CHRONOLOGY OF NAME CHANGES

1867 - Saint Augustine's Normal School and Collegiate Institute
1893 - Saint Augustine's School
1919 - Saint Augustine's Junior College
1928 - Saint Augustine's College

LOCATION

The college is located in the Raleigh-Durham area, which is in the central part of North Carolina. The airport is 15 miles from the campus and passenger rail service is less than a mile from campus.

The Address: **Saint Augustine's College**
1315 Oakwood Avenue
Raleigh, North Carolina 27611
Telephone: (919) 828-4451

THE INSTITUTION

The college has an average enrollment of 1800 students and offers housing to accommodate seventy-five percent of the student body. The student/faculty ratio is fifteen-to-one. The campus is spread over 110 acres. The structure of the academic program consists of five divisions:

- Business
- Humanities
- Education
- Natural Sciences
- Social Sciences

Each division has its own faculty and offers a choice of majors leading to either the Bachelor of Arts or the Bachelor of Science degree.

For the Bachelor of Arts degree, the majors provided include art, communication media, education, English, history and government, language arts, music, political science, psychology, social studies, social welfare, and urban studies.

For the Bachelor of Science degree, the majors provided are accounting, biology, business, chemistry, computer science, criminal justice, economics, health and physical education, industrial hygiene and safety, mathematics, medical technology, physics, physical therapy, civil engineering, electrical engineering, materials engineering, aerospace engineering, mechanical engineering, industrial engineering, biological and agricultural engineering, chemical engineering, and pre-medicine.

FEES

Cost per academic year: tuition, room and board $3600.

DISTINGUISHED ALUMNI

William S. Thompson	-	Senior Judge, Superior Court District of Columbia
Dr. LeVerne McCummings	-	President, Cheney University, (PA)
Dr. Prezell R. Robinson	-	President, St. Augustine's College

SHAW UNIVERSITY

Shaw University is a private institution affiliated with the Baptist Church and founded in 1865. The first instruction at the postsecondary level was offered in 1874. The first baccalaureate degree was awarded in 1878.

CHRONOLOGY OF NAME CHANGES

1865	-	Raleigh Institute
1870	-	Shaw Collegiate Institute
1875	-	Shaw University

LOCATION

The university is located in Raleigh, the capital city of North Carolina. The campus is less than 60 miles from the Virginia state border. Location in the capital city ensures the campus of a mass transit bus system, an airport with easy accessibility and passenger rail service less than two miles from campus.

The Address: **Shaw University**
118 East South Street
Raleigh, North Carolina 27602
Telephone: (919) 546-8200

THE INSTITUTION

Shaw has an average enrollment of 1500 students and provides on-campus housing for 60 percent of the student body. The student/faculty ratio is twenty-five-to-one and students are provided the opportunity to study abroad in the Middle Eastern countries.

Degrees are offered in the following areas: accounting, business administration, communication, computer science, criminal justice, drama, education, health and physical education, mathematics, music, physical therapy, public administration, psychology and sociology.

FEES

Cost per academic year: tuition $3500, room and board $2200.

DISTINGUISHED ALUMNI

James E. Cheek	-	Youngest President of Shaw and Howard Universities
David C. Linton	-	Vice President Black Music Division Warner Communications
Marianne T. Johnson	-	Asst. Director of Admissions Lincoln University (PA)
Dr. Collie Coleman	-	President, Allen University

WINSTON-SALEM STATE UNIVERSITY

Established as an industrial academy in 1892, the first postsecondary level instruction was offered in 1925. The institution awarded the first baccalaureate degree in 1927. It is a public co-educational institution, a constituent of the University of North Carolina.

CHRONOLOGY OF NAME CHANGES

1892	-	Slater Industrial Academy
1925	-	Winston-Salem Teacher College
1963	-	Winston-Salem State College
1969	-	Winston-Salem State University

LOCATION

The 94-acre campus is located in Winston-Salem, about 70 miles north of Charlotte. Winston-Salem is a relatively large metropolitan area served by a mass transit bus system and two airports.

The Address: **Winston-Salem State University**
601 Martin Luther King, Jr. Dr.
Winston-Salem, North Carolina 27110
Telephone: (919) 750-2000

THE INSTITUTION

The university has an average enrollment of 2600 students, fifty-five percent of these students can be housed on campus. The student/faculty ratio is fifteen-to-one.

The bachelor degree is awarded in accounting, biology, business administration, chemistry, mass communications, computer science, economics, education, English, art, history, mathematics, medical technology, music, nursing, physical education, political science, psychology, radio/TV/film, social welfare, sociology and urban planning.

FEES

Cost per academic year: tuition $3500, room and board $2500.

DISTINGUISHED ALUMNI

Dr. Calvert H. Smith	-	President, Morris Brown College
Dr. Thomas Monteiro	-	Chairman, School of Education, Brooklyn College
Joyce Owens Pettis	-	Asst. Professor of English North Carolina State Univ.

Ohio

2 H/PBCUs

CENTRAL STATE UNIVERSITY

The University was originally chartered in 1887 as a department of Wilberforce University. The first instruction at the postsecondary level was in 1888. The college became a four-year institution in 1941.

CHRONOLOGY OF NAME CHANGES

1887	-	Combined Normal and Industrial Department of Wilberforce University
1941	-	College of Education and Industrial Arts
1951	-	Central State College
1965	-	Central State University

LOCATION

The 60-acre campus is located in Wilberforce, Ohio. It is approximately an equal distance from the cities of Cincinnati, Dayton, and the capitol - Columbus. Cincinnati (50 miles northwest of the campus) is the nearest metropolitan area. All modes of transportation are available to the campus and the university's proximity to the large cities makes for a very active environment.

The Address: **Central State University**
                 Wilberforce, Ohio 45384
                 Telephone: (513) 376-6332

THE INSTITUTION

Central State is a co-educational state-supported institution with an average enrollment of 2500 students and a student/faculty ratio of twenty-to-one. On-campus residence halls house 80 percent of the student body.

Academically, the institution is divided into four colleges:
- College of Arts and Sciences
- Business Administration
- Education
- University College

The University College monitors the academic progress of the incoming student.

The college offers degrees in:
- Biological Science
- Communications
- Education
- Fine and Applied Arts
- Home Economics
- Physical Sciences
- Public Affairs/Services
- Water Resources Management
- Business and Management
- Computer/Info. Sciences
- Engineering Sciences
- Foreign Language
- Mathematics
- Psychology
- Social Sciences

In addition to traditional degree programs, certificates in African-American studies and inter-disciplinary programs in the allied health fields are available.

The dual-degree program in engineering is available with Wright State University. The associate and the bachelor's degrees are offered by the university.

FEES

Cost per academic year: tuition, room and board $6500.

DISTINGUISHED ALUMNI

Leontyne Price	-	Prima Donna
Clay Dixon	-	Mayor, Dayton Ohio
		Elected 1987
John W. Shannon	-	Asst. Secretary of the Army, 1985
Joshua Smith	-	Founder/CEO, The Maxima Corp.
Don H. Barden	-	CEO Barden Cablevision
Dr. Arthur E. Thomas	-	Alumnus, President
		Central State University

WILBERFORCE UNIVERSITY

Wilberforce University is a private institution affiliated with the African Methodist Episcopal Church. It was established in 1843 and issued the first postsecondary instruction in1856. The first baccalaureate was awarded in 1857. It has the destinction of being the oldest predominantly Black private university in the United States.

CHRONOLOGY OF NAME CHANGES

1843	-	Ohio African University
1856	-	Wilberforce University of the Methodist Episcopal Church
1863	-	Wilberforce University

LOCATION

Wilberforce is located 20 miles from Dayton, the nearest metropolitan area. It is approximately 65 miles from both Cincinnati (to the southeast) and the capital, Columbus (to the northwest). An airport is less than 30 miles from campus and passenger rail service is 22 miles away.

The Address: **Wilberforce University**
Wilberforce, Ohio 45384-1091
Telephone: (513) 376-2911

THE INSTITUTION

The average enrollment at the college is 800 and the on-campus housing can accommodate 90 percent of the student body. The student/faculty ratio is twenty-to-one.

The baccalaureate degree is offered in accounting, art/advertising, biology, chemistry, communications, economics, English, finance/banking, health care administration, mathematics, physical science, political science/government, psychology, social welfare work, and sociology. Additionally, the dual-degree program in engineering and computer science is offered in conjunction with the University of Dayton.

FEES

Cost per academic year: tuition $4500, room and board $3000.

DISTINGUISHED ALUMNI

Hattie Q. Brown	-	Founder and President Ohio State Federation of Women and National Association of Colored Women
Floyd Flake	-	1st Full-term African-American Congressman from the 6th Congressional District
Bayard Rustin	-	Activist, Botherhood of Sleeping Car Porters
Orchid I. Johnson	-	Political Activist Founder, Freedom Inc. State Representative, 25th District, Missouri

 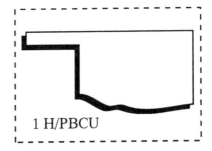

1 H/PBCU

LANGSTON UNIVERSITY

The state-controlled land-grant institution offered its first postsecondary instruction in 1897 and the first baccalaureate was awarded in 1901.

CHRONOLOGY OF NAME CHANGES

    1897 - Colored Agricultural and Normal University
    1941 - Langston University

LOCATION

Located 45 miles from Oklahoma City (the state capital and largest city), and 90 miles from Tulsa (the state's largest oil refining center), the university is readily accessible to all forms of transportation.

The Address: **Langston University**
                P.O. Box 907
                Langston, Oklahoma 73050
                Telephone: (405) 466-2231

The Address: **Cheyney University of Pennsylvania**
Cheyney, Pennsylvania 19319
Telephone: (215) 399-2000

THE INSTITUTION

The 275-acre campus combines modern and traditional architecture providing an environment that encourages serious studying for the more than 1500 students. On-campus students live in five dormitories which can accommodate fifty-five percent of the student body. This public co-educational school offers opportunity for students to achieve a well-rounded education by combining superior academic programs with rich and varied student activities outside the classroom. Cheyney is part of the 14 Universities run by the Pennsylvania State System of Higher Education.

The college has an athletic program that consists of nine sports. The women's basketball team competes in NCAA Division I level. Cheyney offers the bachelor's degree in accounting, art, biology business, chemistry, communication, computer science, drama, earth science, economics, education, English, health and physical education, history, home economics, hotel/restaurant management, industrial arts, language arts, marine science, mathematics, music, nutrition, police science, psychology, social science and urban affairs. Graduate programs include Master of Arts, Master of Science and Master of Education. Dual-degree programs are offered with Meharry for biosciences and Pennsylvania College of Podiatry for podiatry.

FEES

Cost per academic year: tuition, room and board $7000.

DISTINGUISHED ALUMNI

Robert Woodson - President, National Center for
                  Neighborhood Enterprise

Ed Bradley   - Co-host, CBS News Program
                  "60 Minutes"

Martin Ryder   - Director, Secondary Education Program
                  Norfolk State College

Andre Waters   - Pro-football player, Philadelphia Eagles

Marvin Frazier   - Pro-football player, Denver, Broncos

Yolanda Laney & - Kodak All-American Basketball
Valerie Walker   players

Rosalyn T. Jones - Professor, Albany State College

LINCOLN UNIVERSITY (PA)

Lincoln was the first college established in the United States to have, as its original purpose, the higher education of youth of African descent. The university was founded by a Presbyterian Minister and as late as the 1900s, only accepted whites on its faculty. It was established and chartered as Ashmun Institute and offered the first instruction at the postsecondary level in 1854. It was renamed in honor of slain president, Abraham Lincoln. The first baccalaureate was awarded in 1868.

CHRONOLOGY OF NAME CHANGES

1854 - Ashmun Institute
1866 - Lincoln University

LOCATION

Lincoln University is surrounded by rolling farmlands and wooded hilltops of southern Chester county, Pennsylvania. Philadelphia, the largest metropolitan area, is forty-five miles south of campus. Oxford, the town nearest the campus is four miles south. A mass transit bus system, an airport (90 miles away) and passenger rail service (50 miles away) make access to the campus relatively easy.

The Address: **Lincoln University**
Old Route 1
Lincoln University, Pennsylvania 19532
Telephone: (215) 932-8300

THE INSTITUTION

The university has an average enrollment of 1200 students on a campus that occupies 422 acres. The student/faculty ratio is fifteen-to-one. The dormitories, a part of the 27 major buildings, provide on-campus housing for 90 percent of the students. A dual-program in engineering with Drexel University, Lafayette College, Pennsylvania State University and in international service with American University are among the options available for students. Academic degrees awarded are the associate, bachelor's and master's degrees. Students can participate in study abroad programs in Brazil, Canada, France, Mexico, Spain, Taiwan and Russia.

Majors are offered in accounting, biology, business, chemistry, computer science, economics, education, English, health and physical education, history, human services, languages, music, philosophy, physics, political science, psychology, public administration, religion, social science and sociology/anthropology. The Lincoln Advanced Science and Engineering Reinforcement Program (LASER) is recognized as one of the most successful in the nation.

A special honors program emphasizing attention to global, social issues and the critical languages and cultures–Russian, Chinese, Arabic and Japanese–is available. To participants in this program, students must have SAT scores above 850 and a 3.0 GPA.

FEES

Cost per academic year: tuition $4100, room and board $2700.

DISTINGUISHED ALUMNI

Thurgood Marshall	-	1st African-American Justice of the United States Supreme Court Justice
Wilbert A. Tatum	-	Publisher, Editor-In-Chief Amsterdam News
Langston Hughes	-	World acclaimed poet

James L. Usry	-	1st African-American Mayor of Atlantic City
Kwame Nkrumah	-	1st Prime Minister and 1st President of Ghana
Franklin H. Williams	-	Former Ambassador to United Nations and Ghana
Nnamdi Azikiwe	-	1st President of Nigeria
Roscoe Lee Browne	-	Author/Actor of Stage and Screen

The university has also graduated 37 college presidents, 20 percent of the African-American physicians and 10 percent of the African-American lawyers in the nation.

South Carolina

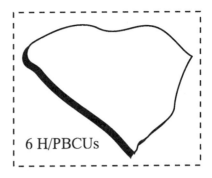

6 H/PBCUs

ALLEN UNIVERSITY

Allen University, the oldest African-American college in South Carolina, was founded in 1870. It is a private church-related school operated by the African Methodist Episcopal Church.

LOCATION

The University is located in the beautiful city of Columbia, the capital city of South Carolina. All modern means of transportation, air, rail, bus and private car service the area.

The Address: **Allen University**
1530 Harden Street
Columbia, South Carolina 29204
Telephone: (803) 254-4165

THE INSTITUTION

The private co-educational institution is situated on 21 acres and has 18 major buildings. Five of these buildings have been officially awarded the "Historic District Status" by the U.S. Department of Interior. The university cites as its major objective, to make

---

available for all students, a substantial and organized curriculum in general education. The university lists among its affiliations the American Association of Colleges for Teacher Education, the National Business Education Association and American Association of College Athletic Directors.

There are four major academic divisions:
- Education
- Humanities
- Natural Sciences
- Behavioral Sciences

The baccalaureate degree is awarded in the following disciplines: art, biology, business administration, elementary education, English, gerontology, health and physical education, mathematics and music performance, religion/theology, social science, social work and sociology.

Allen has an enrollment of 700 with a student/faculty ratio of eleven-to-one.

FEES

Cost per academic year: tuition, room and board $6000.

DISTINGUISHED ALUMNI

The college has produced ten college presidents, including Dr. W. Dean Goldsby, President, Shorter College, Little Rock, Arkansas.

BENEDICT COLLEGE

Established as Benedict Institute in 1870, the founders of the college were affiliated with the Baptist Church. The college provided the first instruction at the postsecondary level in 1889.

CHRONOLOGY OF NAME CHANGES

    1870 - Benedict Institute
    1984 - Benedict College

LOCATION

Benedict College is located in the heart of South Carolina's capital city, Columbia, and is within walking distance of any place in the downtown area. The city offers a wide variety of leisure activities and historical attractions, a strong support of the arts, as well as quality shopping and dining.

The Address: **Benedict College**
                 Harden and Blanding Streets
                 Columbia, South Carolina 29204
                 Telephone: (803) 253-5120
                 1-800-868-6598

THE INSTITUTION

Benedict is a co-educational private independent college. It occupies 20 aces in Columbia, South Carolina. The 1500 students at Benedict enjoy a student/faculty ratio of seventeen-to-one. The college offers majors in four divisions.
- Division of Business
- Division of Mathematics and Natural Sciences
- Division of Humanities
- Division of Social and Behavioral Sciences

Degrees are awarded in accounting, arts, biology, business, chemistry, economics, English, health and physical education, history, marine sociology. The Bachelor of Arts, Bachelor of Science and the Bachelor of Social Work degrees are awarded. A dual-degree in engineering with Georgia Tech. and Southern Technical Institute, and in medicine and dentistry with University of South Carolina, is available.

FEES

Cost per academic year: tuition, room and board $7000.

DISTINGUISHED ALUMNI

Dr. Luns C. Richardson	-	President, Morris College
Dr. Jacqueline D. Myers	-	Business Professor
		Alabama State College

CLAFLIN COLLEGE

Claflin was chartered and offered its first instruction at the postsecondary level in 1869. The private co-educational institution, founded by William and Lee Claflin, is affiliated with the United Methodist Church.

LOCATION

The college is located about 30 miles from the capital city of Columbia and a short distance from Lake Marion. The 25-acre tract of land is near the business district of Orangeburg.

The Address: **Claflin College**
                College Avenue Northeast
                Orangeburg, South Carolina 29115
                Telephone: (803) 534-2710

THE INSTITUTION

The Claflin campus has approximately 1000 students and a student/ faculty ratio of thirteen-to-one. On campus housing is available to the students on a first-come first-served basis. The baccalaureate degree is offered in art, biology, business administration, chemistry, education, English, history, mathematics, and computer science, music physical education, religion and philosophy, social studies and sociology.

The degrees granted are Bachelor of Arts, Bachelor of Science and Bachelor of Science in Education.

FEES

Cost per academic year: tuition, room and board $6500.

DISTINGUISHED ALUMNI

Ernest A. Finney Jr.	-	Assoc. Justice, South Carolina Supreme Court
Jonas P. Kennedy, M.D.	-	Millionaire Turkey Farmer
Bishop Joseph Bethea	-	S.C. Conference of United Methodist Church
Robert L. Alford, Ph.D.	-	Director of Testing Norfolk State University
Mary Honor Wright	-	Educator, established several educational schools in Spartanburg, S.C.

MORRIS COLLEGE

The college was established in 1908 in association with the Baptist Educational and Missionary Convention of South Carolina. It was incorporated and offered first postsecondary level instruction in 1911 and awarded the first baccalaureate degree in 1915.

LOCATION

The campus is located 30 miles east of Columbia, the capital of South Carolina. The nearest airport is 60 miles from campus and rail service is 40 miles from campus. Bus or car provide easy access to the campus. The town of Sumter has a population of 25,000.

The Address: **Morris College**
North Main Street
Sumter, South Carolina 29150
Telephone: (803) 775-9371

THE INSTITUTION

Morris College is a private co-educational church-affiliated institution with an average student enrollment of 700 and a student/ faculty ratio of twenty-to-one. On-campus residence halls house seventy-three percent of the student body.

The college is divided into four divisions:

- Education
- Humanities
- Natural Sciences and Mathematics
- Social Sciences

Majors are available in accounting, allied health, biology, business administration, computer sciences and information, education, English, fine arts, gerontology, history, mathematics, military science, music, religion , social science and sociology.

FEES

Cost per academic year: tuition, room and board $6500.

DISTINGUISHED ALUMNI

Dr. Arthenia Bates Millican   - Former English Professor
                              Southern University
Dr. Ralph W. Canty   - Past President, National
                              Progressive Baptist Convention
                              Member, House of Represen-
                              tatives, S.C. District 66
Dr. Gaosen Tarieton   - Physician, Nashville, TN
James Solomon   - State Commissioner
                              Social Services Department

SOUTH CAROLINA STATE COLLEGE

South Carolina State College is a public co-educational institution founded in 1896.

LOCATION

South Carolina State is located approximately 60 miles from Charleston and less than 70 miles from the ocean. Students attending the college have access to the beautiful gardens of Charleston and the famed tropical Cypress Gardens. The nearest airport is in the metropolitan city of Charleston.

The Address: **South Carolina State College**
P.O. Box 1568
Orangeburg, South Carolina 29117
Telephone: (803) 536-7000 and 536-7185

THE INSTITUTION

Located on 147 acres, the campus has 60 buildings and 12 dormitories which house 60 percent of the 4400 students. The student/faculty ratio is twenty-to-one. The baccalaureate degree is offered in the following areas:

- Bachelor of Arts: art (printmaking), drama, English, French, history, political science, sociology, Spanish, speech pathology, social studies and music.

- Bachelor of Science: accounting, agri-business, biology, business, chemistry, computer science, criminal justice, economics, engineering, foods and nutrition, health education, home economics, industrial education, mathematics, nursing, physical education, physics, psychology, and social welfare.

FEES

Cost per academic year: tuition, room and board $6000.

DISTINGUISHED ALUMNI

Dr. Emily M. Chapman - Administrator, Urban Center Lincoln University (PA)

Eric M. Westbury - Asst. President, First Union National Bank of South Carolina

Marianna W. Davis - 1st Woman to serve on South Carolina Commission on Higher Education

James O. Heyward - Director of Admission Alabama A & M University

Veryl Scott, J.D. - Business Department Administrator, Norfolk Univ.

VOORHEES COLLEGE

Voorhees College was established in 1897 as a private college affiliated with the Episcopal Church. It was the first historically Black institution of higher learning in South Carolina to achieve full accreditation by the Southern Association of Colleges and Schools. The college was founded by a young African-American woman, Ms. Elizabeth Evelyn Wright who was determined to start a school for Black youth.

CHRONOLOGY OF NAME CHANGES

1897	-	Denmark Industrial School
1902	-	Voorhees Industrial School
1929	-	Voorhees Normal and Industrial School
1947	-	Voorhees School and Junior College
1962	-	Voorhees College

LOCATION

Voorhees College is located less than two miles east of Denmark, South Carolina, on 350 acres. It is 45 miles south of Columbia, the state capital, which is the nearest metropolitan area. The airport is 50 miles from campus and passenger rail service is two miles from campus.

The Address: **Voorhees College**
Denmark, South Carolina 29042
Telephone: (803) 793-3351

THE INSTITUTION

The tree-shaded campus provides on-campus housing for seventy-nine percent of the student enrollment which averages 600. Historic St. Philip's Episcopal Chapel is located on the academic circle of the campus and was built in 1935 entirely by Voorhees students. The student/faculty ratio is fifteen-to-one.

Voorhees College offers degree at two levels: associate, baccalaureate and pre-professional programs in Engineering and law. Major concentrations are offered within each of the four academic divisions as follows:

DIVISION OF BUSINESS AND ECONOMICS
- Accounting, business administration, business education, office administration

DIVISION OF EDUCATION AND HUMANITIES
- Elementary education, English education, English communications

DIVISION OF NATURAL SCIENCES, MATHEMATICS, AND COMPUTER SCIENCE
- Biology, chemistry, computer science, mathematics

DIVISION OF SOCIAL SCIENCES
- Criminal justice, sociology, social work, social studies education, political science

FEES

Cost per academic year: tuition, room and board $6000.

DISTINGUISHED ALUMNI

Leonard Spring	-	Vice President, First Union Bank, Charlotte, N.C.
Dr. Prezell Robinson	-	President, St. Augustine's College
Jerry M. Screen	-	Attorney-at-Law

Tennessee

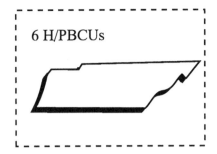

6 H/PBCUs

FISK UNIVERSITY

Fisk University, founded in 1866, is a private co-educational liberal arts institution. The first postsecondary instruction was offered in 1871 and the first baccalaureate degree was awarded in 1875. Fisk was the first historically Black college to gain full accreditation by the Southern Association of Colleges and Schools. Additionally, it was the first historically Black college to be awarded university status.

CHRONOLOGY OF NAME CHANGES

    1866 -   Fisk School
    1967 -   Fisk University

LOCATION

Fisk is located two miles from downtown Nashville. Being located in the capital and second largest city in Tennessee, students have access to a part of the rich history of the south. The 46-acre campus has 28 major buildings and is listed in the national historic registry. There are 17 other colleges nearby.

All major forms of transportation are available to the campus.

The Address: **Fisk University**
                1000 17th Avenue, North
                Nashville, Tennessee 37203
                Telephone: (615) 329-8665

INSTITUTION

The enrollment at the campus averages 800 with a student/faculty ratio of eleven-to-one. Fisk is part of the Nashville University and Meharry Medical College, which permits students to attend classes at these institutions while enrolled at Fisk. The following dual-degree or joint programs are offered: science and engineering with Vanderbilt; science and pharmacy with Howard University; elementary education with George Peabody College; nursing and medical technology with Rush-Presbyterian-St. Luke Medical Center in Chicago, Illinois, and the Master of Business Administration with Owen School of Management at Vanderbilt University. The opportunity to participate in ROTC is available with Vanderbilt and Tennessee State University.

Fisk students may participate in a number of extra-curricular activities including the Fisk Jubilee Singers, the Orchesis Dance Club, the Stagecrafters, Greek letter fraternities and sororities, and intramural and intercollegiate athletics.

The library is noted for its special collections such as: The Negro Collection which includes works of Langston Hughes and W.E. B. Dubois; the Black Oral History Collection and the George Gershwin Collection of Music. Additionally, the university has one of the most outstanding art galleries in any southern school with the Steiglitz Collection donated by Georgia O'keeffe, and paintings of Cezanne and Renoir.

The academic program offers liberal arts and pre-professional programs leading to the Bachelor of Arts, Bachelor of Science and Master of Arts degrees. The major departments are:

- Humanities and Fine Arts
- Natural Sciences and Mathematics
- Social Sciences
- Business Administration

In the graduate studies area:

- Biology
- Chemistry
- Physics
- Psychology
- Sociology

FEES

Cost per academic year: tuition, room and board $6000.

DISTINGUISHED ALUMNI

William Edward Burgharot Du Bois-	Historian, Scholar Educator, Founder of Niagara Movement, a precursor of NAACP
Wilhelmina Delco	- Speaker Pro Tempore State of Texas
Margaret James Murray Washington-	1st Dean of Women Tuskegee Institute
John Hope Franklin	- Historian, Educator
Roland Hayes	- Professional Singer
Hortense Golden Canady	- Past National President Delta Sigma Theta Sorority

KNOXVILLE COLLEGE

Knoxville is a private college affiliated with the United Presbyterian Church. The college was established in 1863 as a school for Negro youth. The first postsecondary level instruction was offered in 1877 and the first baccalaureate degree was awarded in 1883.

CHRONOLOGY OF NAME CHANGES

```
1863  -  McKee School for Negro Youth
1875  -  Knoxville College
```

LOCATION

Located in the eastern part of Tennessee and close to the Great Smoky Mountain National Park, Knoxville college is 20 miles north of Oak Ridge (headquarters for Tennessee Valley Authority and the American Museum of Atomic Energy). There is mass transit available, and the city is easily accessible by air or rail transportation.

The Address: **Knoxville College**
901 College Street W
Knoxville, Tennessee 37921
Telephone: (615) 524-6525

THE INSTITUTION

The 50-acre campus has an average enrollment of 500 students and offers the associate and bachelor's degrees. Campus housing is available for fifty-two percent of the student body. The student/faculty ratio is twelve-to-one. Intercollegiate athletics is a part of the activities available to the students. The major areas of concentrations are biological sciences, business and management, communications, education, fine and applied arts, mathematics, psychology and social sciences.

FEES

Cost per academic year: tuition $4800, room $3400, board $1250.

DISTINGUISHED ALUMNI

Johnnie Ford   - Mayor of Tuskegee
Dr. John E. Reinhardt   - U.S. Ambassador to Liberia
Dr. Herman Smith   - Former Chancellor, University of Arkansas in Pine Bluff
Edith Irvy   - 1st African-American to take medical training at Arkansas University
Melvyn L. Burroughs, Ph.D. - Director of Housing Lincoln University (PA)

LANE COLLEGE

Originally established in 1882 as a high school to teach Colored children, the institute awarded its first baccalaureate degree in 1899. Lane College, named for Bishop Isaac Lane, is a private institution affiliated with the Christian Methodist Episcopal Church.

CHRONOLOGY OF NAME CHANGES

1882 - Colored Methodist Episcopal High School
1883 - Lane Institute
1895 - Lane College

LOCATION

The college is located in the western part of Tennessee between Memphis, the largest city in the state, and Nashville, the capital and second largest city in the state. A bus system and passenger rail service provide transportation to the campus.

The Address: **Lane College
545 Lane Avenue
Jackson, Tennessee 38301
Telephone: (901) 424-4600**

THE INSTITUTE

Lane College is a small fifteen-acre campus with an average enrollment of 600 students. On-campus housing is available for eighty-five percent of the student body. The student/faculty ratio is fifteen-to-one. A dual-degree program in computer science with Jackson State University and in engineering with Tennessee State University is available. The college is divided into five major divisions—Education, General Studies, Humanities, Natural Sciences and Social Sciences. The Bachelor of Arts and the Bachelor of Science degrees are offered in a variety of areas including biological sciences, business and management, chemistry, communication, computer and information sciences, education, English, mathematics, music, physical education and sociology.

FEES

Cost per academic year: tuition $3500, room and boar: $3000.

DISTINGUISHED ALUMNI

Otis L. Floyd Jr.	-	President, Tennessee State Univ.
David H. Johnson	-	President, Texas College

LeMOYNE-OWEN COLLEGE

The College was established in 1871 as a private school affiliated with the United Church of Christ and the Tennessee Baptist Convention. The first postsecondary instructions were offered in 1924 and the first baccalaureate degree was awarded in 1932.

CHRONOLOGY OF NAME CHANGES

1871 - LeMoyne Normal and Commercial School
1934 - LeMoyne College
1965 - LeMoyne-Owen College

LOCATION

LeMoyne-Owen is located in the largest city in Tennessee and provides the students with all the benefits of a large metropolitan city: mass transit bus system, air and passenger rail service, shopping malls, theaters, etc.

The Address: **LeMoyne-Owen College**
807 Walker Avenue
Memphis, Tennessee 38126
Telephone: (901) 942-7302

THE INSTITUTION

The fifteen-acre campus has an average enrollment of 1000 students and a student/faculty ratio of twenty-to-one. The school has a mandatory cooperative education program, offers the dual-degree program in engineering with Christian Brothers College and Tuskegee University, and provides for study abroad in France, Mexico and other countries by individual arrangement.

Study programs are available in the following areas: accounting, biological sciences, business and management, computer and information sciences, fine and applied arts, history, humanities, mathematics, natural sciences, occupational therapy, physical therapy, political science, and social sciences.

The institute awards the Bachelor of Arts, Bachelor of Business Administration and the Bachelor of Science.

LeMoyne-Owen is a commuter college. There are no dormitories on campus.

FEES

Cost per academic year: tuition $4500.

DISTINGUISHED ALUMNI

    Benjamin Lawson Hooks J.D. - Executive Director, NAACP
    Marian S. Barry   - Former Mayor
                                 Washington, D.C.
    Eric C. Lincoln Ph.D LLD   - Consultant, Change
                                 Magazine, Professor
                                 Duke University

MEHARRY MEDICAL COLLEGE

Founded in 1876 as the Medical Department of Central Tennessee College, the school was reorganized as Walden University and the Medical Department became Meharry Medical College of Walden University. Five years later, the college was established as a separate corporation and has remained so since that time.

CHRONOLOGY OF NAME CHANGES

1876	-	Medical Department of Central Tennessee College
1900	-	Walden University
1905	-	Meharrry Medical College

LOCATION

Meharry is located in Nashville, Tennessee. The campus is in the northern section of the city, close to two other historically Black colleges, Fisk and Tennessee State University.

Transportation in the area is provided by a mass transit bus system, an airport and passenger rail service.

The Address: **Meharry Medical College**
1005 - D.B. Todd Blvd.
Nashville, Tennessee 37208
Telephone: (615) 327-6111

THE INSTITUTION

The 62-acre private co-educational institution has an enrollment of 700 students. There is no on-campus housing, however, on-campus residence halls are available. The student/faculty ratio is six-to-one.

The institution is composed of four schools:
- School of Medicine
- School of Dentistry
- School of Graduate Studies
- School of Allied Health

and the George W. Hubbard Hospital.

The graduate degrees awarded are Master of Science, Doctor of Medicine, Doctor of Dental Surgery, and Doctor of Philosophy.

FEES

Cost per academic year: tuition $15,000.

DISTINGUISHED ALUMNI

Alma Rose George, M.D. -	Surgeon and President Medical Staff, Mercy Hospital, Detroit
Robert D. Miller Jr. M.D. -	1984 President, Arkansas State Board of Health
Jacob L. Shirley -	Director, Health Services Albany State College
Marion Perry Bowers -	Member Meharry's Upper Tenth Former Chief Otolaryngology Service, AUS General Hospital Frankfurt, Germany

TENNESSEE STATE UNIVERSITY

Tennessee State was founded in 1912 as a public land grant co-educational institution. In 1979 it merged with the University of Tennessee at Nashville.

CHRONOLOGY OF NAME CHANGES

1912 - Tennessee Agriculture & Industrial State Normal School for Negroes

1979 - Tennessee State University

LOCATION

The College is located in Nashville, the capital and second-largest city in Tennessee. It is served by a mass-transit system, passenger rail service and airport service.

The Address: **Tennessee State University**
3500 Centennial Blvd.
Nashville, Tennessee 37203
Telephone: (615) 320-3131

THE INSTITUTION

Tennessee State has an enrollment that averages 8000 and a student/faculty ratio of eighteen-to-one. The main campus has 50 buildings, including dormitories on 515 acres.

The bachelor degree is offered in the following majors: agriculture, allied arts, allied health fields, animal science, architecture, arts and science, biological   sciences, biology, business administration, chemistry, communications, computer science, counseling/student personnel, dental hygiene, drama, economics, education, engineering, English, foreign language, health care administration, history, home economics, industrial administration/relations, mathematics, medical records administration, music, nursing, physics, political science, psychology, public administration, reading, recreation/leisure, respiration therapy, rural development, sociology and speech correction.

The degrees offered are Associate in Applied Science, Bachelor of Science, Bachelor of Science in Nursing, Master of Arts, Master of Arts in Education, Master of Business Administration, Master of Criminal Justice, Master of Engineering, Master of Public Administration, Specialist in Education, Doctor of Education, and Doctor of Philosophy.

During the freshman and sophomore years, all students are enrolled in the University College to complete the general education requirements and to explore career goals before declaring a major.

FEES

Cost per academic year: tuition, room and board $6000.

DISTINGUISHED ALUMNI

Oprah Winfrey	-	Television Star and Producer
Wilma Rudolph	-	Olympic Gold medalist -Track
Hazo W. Carter, Jr.	-	9th President, West Virginia State
Brenda F. Savage	-	Assoc. Professor, Lincoln Univ. (PA)
Dick Griffey	-	CEO Dick Griffey Productions (CA)

Azie Taylor Morton
Huston-Tilloston College graduate

—First African-American woman
to sign her name to U.S. currency

Texas

7 H/PBCUs

HUSTON-TILLOTSON COLLEGE

Established as Tillotson Collegiate and Normal Institute in 1875, it was chartered in 1877. The first postsecondary instruction was offered in 1881. The first baccalaureate was awarded in 1909 and it became a four-year college in 1931. The college merged with Samuel Huston College in 1952.

CHRONOLOGY OF NAME CHANGES

    1875 -   Tillotson Collegiate and Normal Institute
    1879 -   Tillotson College
    1952 -   Huston-Tillotson College

LOCATION

Austin (the location of the campus) was the national capital until Texas became a state. Austin is now the capital city of Texas. The twenty-three-acre campus is served by mass transit bus system, an airport five miles from campus and passenger rail service three miles away.

State: TEXAS   **193**

The Address: **Huston-Tillotson College**
1820 East 8th Street
Austin, Texas 78702
Telephone: (512) 476-7421

THE INSTITUTION

Huston-Tillotson is a private co-educational college affiliated with the United Methodist Church and the United Church of Christ. It has an average enrollment of 500 students and offers a varied curriculum awarding the bachelor's to those who complete the program. On-campus housing can accommodate forty-seven percent of the students.

The college is divided into four academic divisions:
* Education
* Humanities
* Natural Sciences
* Social Sciences

Bachelor's degrees have been awarded in the following areas: biological sciences, business management, computer and information sciences, education, mathematics, physical sciences, and social sciences. Intercollegiate sports are offered for men and women.

FEES

Cost per academic year: tuition $3200, room $1000, board $2000

DISTINGUISHED ALUMNI

Honorable Leonard H. Robinson, Jr. - Deputy Asst. Sec't of State, African Affairs, State Dept.
Azie Taylor Morton - 36th U.S. Treasurer

JARVIS CHRISTIAN COLLEGE

Jarvis Christian is a private liberal arts college affiliated with the Christian Church (Disciples of Christ). The recorded history begins in 1904 when Mary Alphin and the Christian Woman's Board of Missions began to plan for a school for Black youth. In 1910, land near Hawkins, Texas, was donated by Major J.J. Jarvis. Initially an elementary school, the school was incorporated as a college in 1928. Senior college courses were introduced in 1937. The first baccalaureate degree was awarded in 1939.

CHRONOLOGY OF NAME CHANGES

    1912 -   Jarvis Christian Institute
    1937 -   Jarvis Christian College

LOCATION

Jarvis Christian is located one mile east of Hawkins, Texas. The campus is situated in an attractive wooded area of about 1000 acres. The major industry in the area is the college. Most of the residents of the town are associated with the college. Tyler is 20 miles south of the campus and the nearest metropolitan area is Dallas, 130 miles from campus. Airline service to the Dallas-Fort Worth airport is accessible via Interstate 20.

The Address: **Jarvis Christian College**
                  U.S. Highway 80
                  West Drawer G
                  Hawkins, Texas 75765
                  Telephone: (214) 769-2174

THE INSTITUTION

This small co-educational church-related institution of higher education enjoys a student/faculty ratio of ten-to-one. On-campus residence halls house seventy-five percent of the student body, and additional housing is available for married students on a first-come first-served basis. Courses offered are grouped into five divisions and include the following areas:

- DIVISION OF BASIC STUDIES
  - Communications
  - Humanities and Social Sciences
  - Science and Mathematics
- DIVISION OF BUSINESS ADMINISTRATION
- DIVISION OF EDUCATION
  - Secondary Education
  - Elementary Education
  - Physical Education
- DIVISION OF HUMANITIES AND SOCIAL SCIENCE
  - Fine Arts
  - Literature and Language
  - Religion
  - Social and Behavioral Science
- DIVISION OF SCIENCE AND MATHEMATICS
  - Allied Health and Biology
  - Mathematics and Physical Science

Cooperative pre-medical programs with Fisk University and Meharry Medical College are sponsored by the United Negro College Fund Premedical Summer Program. Semester programs at Brookhaven National Laboratory are available for mathematics and science majors.

<u>FEES</u>

Cost per semester: tuition $4200, room $1000, board $1500.

<u>DISTINGUISHED ALUMNI</u>

Dr. James O. Perpener	-	5th President, Jarvis Christian College
Dr. E. Wadworth Rand	-	7th President, Jarvis Christian College
Dr. C.A. Berry	-	President, Jarvis Christian College

PAUL QUINN COLLEGE

The College was founded in 1872 by a small group of African Methodist circuit-riding preachers in Austin, Texas. The college later moved to the city of Waco where it has served the needs of many youth for nearly 120 years. In 1990, the college moved to Dallas and occupies the campus which was previously Bishop College. It is the oldest predominantly Black liberal arts college in the state of Texas.

LOCATION

The recent move from Waco to Dallas provides students access to one of the most modern cities in America. All modes of transportation are available to the campus.

The Address: **Paul Quinn College**
3837 Simpson Stuart Road
Dallas, Texas 75241
Telephone: (214) 376-1000

THE INSTITUTION

The average enrollment at the college is 400 students, with a student/ faculty ratio of twelve-to-one. The educational program is organized into four academic division:
- Division of Arts and Sciences
- Division of Professional Studies
- Division of Education
- Division of Developmental Studies

The bachelor degree is offered in: accounting, biology, business administration, computer science, criminal justice, economics, education, English, fine arts, foreign languages, gerontology, history/political science, psychology, social work and sociology.

A parallel-degree program with Texas State Technical Institute (TSTI) makes it possible for students to earn an asssociate degree from TSTI and a Bachelor of Applied Science from Paul Quinn College. Nine such specialized programs are available.

Paul Quinn, in cooperation with the Waco Model Cities Community Development Association, established an Ethnic Cultural Center in 1970.

FEES

Cost per academic semester: tuition $1500, room and board $2500.

DISTINGUISHED ALUMNI

Leon Dorsey - Owner, President Dorsey-Keatts Funeral Home, Inc.

PRAIRIE VIEW A & M UNIVERSITY

Prairie View was established as an agricultural school and offered the first instruction at the postsecondary level in 1878. The first baccalaureate degree was awarded in 1902.

CHRONOLOGY OF NAME CHANGES

1876	-	Alta Vista Agriculture College
1895	-	Prairie View Normal and Industrial College
1945	-	Prairie View University
1947	-	Prairie View Agricultural and Mechanical College of Texas
1971	-	Prairie View Agricultural and Mechanical University
1973	-	Prairie View A & M University

LOCATION

The university is situated on a 1440-acre site in Waller County, 40 miles northwest of Houston. It is accessible by major highways and the Houston International Airport. The semi-rural city environment has access to Houston, a major metropolis offering a variety of restaurants, shopping facilities and ethnic festivals.

The Address: **Prairie View A & M University**
P.O. Box 66
Prairie View, Texas 77446-0066
Telephone: 1-800-334-1807

THE INSTITUTION

The enrollment at PV averages 5000 with slightly more men than women. On-campus housing consists of nine residence halls capable of accommodating eighty percent of the students.

The university offers the following undergraduate degrees: the Bachelor of Arts, Bachelor of Arts in Social Work, Bachelor of Architecture, Bachelor of Business Administration, Bachelor of Music and Bachelor of Science in Agriculture, Chemical Engineering, Civil Engineering, Computer Engineering, Technology, Dietetics, Education, Electrical Engineering, Home Economics, Industrial Education and Technology Law Enforcement, Mechanical Engineering and Technology, and Nursing. For the truly motivated students, the Benjamin Banneker Honors College provides the opportunity to excel academically in a positive living/learning setting.

FEES

Cost per academic year: tuition $3000, room and board $3000 to $3600.

DISTINGUISHED ALUMNI

Hobart Taylor Jr.	-	Special Counsel to President L.B. Johnson Board of Directors, Aetna Life & Casuality Co.
Jiles P. Daniels	-	Vice President, Student Affairs Prairie View A & M
Percy E. Sutton	-	Retired, Inner City Broadcasting Corp. (NY)

TEXAS COLLEGE

Established in 1894, Texas College offered its first instruction at the postsecondary level in 1895. The private co-educational school is affiliated with the Christian Methodist Episcopal Church.

CHRONOLOGY OF NAME CHANGES

```
1894  -  Texas College
1901  -  Phillips University
1912  -  Texas College
```

LOCATION

The college is located in Tyler, a town of about 100,000 population. Dallas, the largest and closest metropolitan city, is situated less than 100 miles east of the campus. It is served by mass transit bus system and an airport ten miles away.

The Address: **Texas College**
2404 North Grand Avenue
Tyler, Texas 75702
Telephone: (214) 593-8311

THE INSTITUTION

The average enrollment is 500 on a 15-acre site. On-campus residence halls can accommodate forty-seven percent of the student body. Housing is available for married students. The student/faculty ratio is fifteen-to-one.

Degrees are offered in the following areas: art, biology, business administration, computer science, education, English, history, mathematics, music, physical education, political science, social sciences, social work and sociology.

Course work may be pursued in non-degree subject matter. These fields include: chemistry, drama, economics, French, geography, physics, Spanish, speech, pre-law, pre-medicine and pre-dentistry.

FEES

Cost per academic year: tuition $3200, room and board $2500.

DISTINGUISHED ALUMNI

E. Grace Payne   -   Chairperson, Los Angeles Harbor
                          Commission
Phyllis Buford   -   Administrator, Medgar Evers College
Dr. Jimmy E. Clark   -   President, Texas College

TEXAS SOUTHERN UNIVERSITY

Texas Southern was established and offered its first instruction at the postsecondary level in 1947. The first baccalaureate was awarded in 1948.

CHRONOLOGY OF NAME CHANGES

    1947 - Texas State University
    1951 - Texas Southern University

LOCATION

The campus of 130 acres is located in the heart of Houston, the largest city in Texas and the fourth largest city in the United States. Transportation to the campus is provided by mass bus transit system, passenger rail service and the Houston airport.

The Address: **Texas Southern University**
                   3100 Cleburne Avenue
                   Houston, Texas 77004-9987
                   Telephone: (713) 527-7305 or 527-7011

THE INSTITUTION

Texas Southern University has an average enrollment of 7500 students. Five dormitories provide housing for 11 percent of the student body. Each dormitory is in close proximity to all of the schools and colleges and the student life center. The student/faculty ratio is twenty-five-to-one. There are seven Schools/Colleges comprising the academic program:
- College of Arts and Science
- College of Education
- College of Pharmacy and Health Services

- School of Business
- School of Technology
- Graduate School
- School of Law

The university offers a variety of undergraduate, graduate, and professional degree programs. The basic areas in which degrees may be received are: accounting, administration of justice, airway science, architectural construction technology, art, bilingual education, building construction management, business education, chemistry, child development, computer science, dietetics, drafting and design technology, economics, education, engineering, French, health administration, history, home economics, journalism, mathematics, medical records administration, music, pharmacy, physical education, physics, political science, power and transportation, public administration, respiratory therapy, social work, sociology, Spanish and telecommunication.

The doctorate degree is offered in counselor education, curriculum and instruction, education administration, higher education, urban education, and pharmacy. Professional degree programs are available in accounting, law, pharmacy and social work.

FEES

Cost per academic year: tuition $1800, room $1500, board $1500.

DISTINGUISHED ALUMNI

Barbara C. Jordan Esq.	-	First African-American female elected to the Congress from the South; First African-American female elected to preside over a legislative body.
Craig Washington	-	U.S. Representative, 18th District-Houston, Texas

WILEY COLLEGE

Wiley college was founded by Freedmen's Aid Society in 1873. It is a Christian co-educational institution, affiliated with the United Methodist Church, and named for Bishop Issac W. Wiley. Originally, the college was located in two frame buildings south of Marshall, Texas. In 1880, it moved to its present site. Wiley was the first of the Negro colleges west of the Mississippi River to be granted the "A" rating by the Southern Association of Colleges and Secondary Schools.

LOCATION

The sixty-three-acre campus is home to 400 students. Dallas, the nearest metropolitan area, is approximately 150 miles from the campus. The airport is 40 miles and passenger rail service is two miles from campus.

The Address: **Wiley College**
71 Rosborough Springs Road
Marshall, Texas 75670
Telephone: (214) 938-8341

THE INSTITUTION

Wiley College is a church-related liberal arts institution. The preparation of teachers for elementary and secondary schools has been identified as one of the primary objectives of the college. The small college provides housing for 50 percent of the student body. The academic programs are organized into five major areas:

- HUMANITIES
    - Modern Languages
    - Religion and Philosophy
    - Fine Arts
- BUSINESS AND SOCIAL SCIENCE
    - Business and Economics
    - Hotel and Restaurant Management
    - History, Social Science and Political Science
    - Sociology
    - Nursing Home Administration
- EDUCATION AND TEACHER TRAINING
    - Elementary Education
    - Special Education
    - Early Childhood Education
    - Physical Education
- NATURAL SCIENCES AND MATHEMATICS
    - Biology
    - Mathematics
    - Chemistry
    - Computer Science
- BASIC STUDIES
    - General College Requirements

FEES

Cost per academic year: tuition, room and board $6500.

DISTINGUISHED ALUMNI

James Farmer	-	Previous Asst. Secretary, HEW
Dr. Walter S. McAfee	-	Former Rosenwald Fellow in Nuclear Physics, Cornell Univ. Science Advisor, AMDEL-SA Fort Mon Mouth, NJ
Dr. Thomas W. Cole Jr.	-	President, Atlanta University

Virgin Islands

1 H/PBCU

UNIVERSITY OF THE VIRGIN ISLANDS

The University of the Virgin Islands is a land-grant institution which was established in 1962. It offers unique educational opportunities with many programs incorporating material specific to the Caribbean.

LOCATION

The U.S. Virgin Islands (a U.S. territory located 1100 miles southeast of Miami) is the home of the university. There are two campuses: the main campus on St. Thomas and a smaller campus on St. Croix. The St. Thomas campus, 175 acres, is located three miles west of Charlotte Amalie and overlooks the Caribbean Sea. The St. Croix campus, 125 acres, is located midway between Christiansted and Frederiksted.

The Address: **University of the Virgin Islands**
                 St. Thomas
                 U.S. Virgin Islands 00802
                 Telephone: (809) 776-9200
                            and
                 University of the Virgin Islands
                 RR-02 Box 10,000
                 Kingshill, St. Croix
                 U.S. Virgin Islands 00851
                 Telephone: (809) 778-1620

THE INSTITUTION

The university is small, with approximately 750 full-time and 1800 part-time students. The low student/faculty ratio of ten-to-one allows individual attention. The Bachelor of Arts, Bachelor of Science and the Associate of Arts degrees are offered.

The opportunity to participate in the Caribbean Research Institute and the Agricultural Experimental Station affords students a unique view of local plants and animals, environmental and health problems, geology, weather and oceanographic patterns specific to the Caribbean.

The university does its best to assure that no one is denied an education because of the expense. Approximately 80 percent of the students at the university receive some form of financial aid. Both federal and institutional programs are available, as well as student loans. Special scholarships are available for students with majors in areas especially needed in the Virgin Islands, such as marine biology.

A program of academic enrichment for high school students who are underachieving and who meet specified federal guidelines is also available at the St. Thomas campus.

FEES

Cost per academic semester: tuition, room and board $3200.

DISTINGUISHED ALUMNI

Reginald I. Hodge - Asst. Vice President, Business & Financial Affairs, University of Virgin Islands

Virginia

6 H/PBCUs

HAMPTON UNIVERSITY

The Institute was founded in 1868 by Samuel C. Armstrong. Hampton is a private independent institution. The first instruction at the postsecondary level was offered in 1922. The first baccalaureate degree was awarded in 1926 and the graduate program was added in 1928.

CHRONOLOGY OF NAME CHANGES

    1868 - Hampton Normal and Agricultural Institute
    1930 - Hampton Institute
    1984 - Hampton University

LOCATION

Hampton is located on the southeast coast of Virginia on the beautiful Chesapeake Bay. Norfolk, ten miles from the campus, is the nearest metropolitan area. The campus is reachable by mass transit bus system, an airport is 13 miles away, and passenger rail service is 8 miles from the campus.

The Address: **Hampton University**
                 West Queen Street
                 Hampton, Virginia 23668
                 Telephone: (804) 727-5000

THE INSTITUTION

Hampton is Virginia's only co-educational non-denominational four-year private college. The university, the parent institution, includes Hampton Institute as the undergraduate college, a Graduate College and the College of Continuing Education.

The 47 buildings located on the two-hundred-and-four-acre waterfront campus is home to more than 4500 students, 70 percent of whom are on-campus residents. The student/faculty ratio is eighteen-to-one. The baccalaureate degree is offered at the School of Arts and Letters, School of Business, School of Education, School of Pure and Applied Science, and the School of Nursing. The master's degree is awarded by the graduate college in administration, biology, business, chemistry, communication, computer education, counseling, education, English, environmental science, home economics, mathematics, museum studies, music, nursing, nutrition, physical education, physics and reading.

A dual-degree program is offered in engineering with Old Dominion University. This college's unique offerings include airway science, architecture, radio, T.V. and print journalism, communication disorders and marine science. Additionally, Hampton's nursing program is the oldest continuous baccalaureate nursing program in the State of Virginia.

FEES

Cost per academic year: tuition, room and board $9000.

DISTINGUISHED ALUMNI

Booker T. Washington	-	Founder of Tuskegee University
John L. Henderson	-	7th President, Wilberforce Univ.
Jerry L. Isaac	-	Asst. to the President Lincoln University (PA)
William Brown Muse, Jr.	-	President, Imperial Savings & Loan Assoc., Martinville, VA
Dr. Sallie Allen-Tucker	-	Assoc. Professor University of Wisconsin
Carl Brooks	-	Vice President, Public Utility Service Corp., N.J.

Hampton University alumni have founded ten institutions.

NORFOLK STATE UNIVERSITY

This state institution was originally established as a junior college and a unit of Virginia Union University. The first instruction at the postsecondary level was offered in 1935.

CHRONOLOGY OF NAME CHANGES

1942	-	Norfolk Polytechnic College
1944	-	Virginia State College
1969	-	Norfolk State College
1979	-	Norfolk State University

LOCATION

The 102-acre campus is located in Norfolk, the second largest city in Virginia. It is surrounded by Newport News, Portsmouth, Hampton, and Virginia Beach and is less than 20 miles from the North Carolina border, just in the southeast tip of the state on Chesapeake Bay. The mass transit bus system, an airport ten miles away, and passenger rail service 30 miles away provide easy access to and from the campus.

The Address: **Norfolk State University**
2401 Corprew Avenue
Norfolk, Virginia 23504
Telephone: (804) 683-8396

THE INSTITUTION

Norfolk State is a public co-educational institution, with an average enrollment of 7400 students and a student/faculty ratio of twenty-to-one. On-campus housing can accommodate twenty-six percent of the student body. Cross-registration is available with Hampton

Institute, Christopher Newport College, Tidewater Community College, Thomas Nelson Community College and Old Dominion University.

Majors are available in accounting, audiology, biology, building construction, business education, chemistry, child/family development, computer science/information, drafting/design, economics, education, electronics, engineering, English, fine arts, food science and technology, foreign language, history, hotel and restaurant management, human resources and development, industrial administration/relations, journalism, mathematics, music education, nursing, physical education, physics, political science, reading, speech corrections, trade and industrial technology and urban studies.

FEES

Cost per academic year: tuition $3000, room and board $3000.

DISTINGUISHED ALUMNI

Tim Reid	-	Radio/TV Star
James Sweat	-	CIAA Coach of the Year, 1991
Karl B. Brockenbrough, CPA	-	Senior Account Lincoln Univ. (PA)
Herman E. Valentine	-	Chairman and President Systems Management American Corp.

SAINT PAUL'S COLLEGE

Saint Paul's College was established in 1888 in affiliation with the Protestant Episcopal Church. The first instruction at the postsecondary level was in 1922; the first baccalaureate was awarded in 1944.

CHRONOLOGY

1888	-	Saint Paul's Normal and Industrial School
1941	-	Saint Paul's Polytechnic Institute
1957	-	Saint Paul's College

LOCATION

Saint Paul's is situated near the southeastern border of Virginia, approximately ten miles from the North Carolina border. It is slightly more than 60 miles from Richmond, the state capital, to the north and Norfolk and Portsmouth on the east. It enjoys close proximity to the popular resort, Virginia Beach.

The Address: **Saint Paul's College**
406 Windsor Avenue
Lawrenceville, Virginia 23868-1299
Telephone: (804) 848-3111

THE INSTITUTION

Saint Paul's College is a private institution with an average enrollment of 800. On-campus residence halls house eighty-five percent of the student body. The student/faculty ratio is eighteen-to-one.

The bachelor degree is awarded in the following areas: accounting, biology, business administration, computer information systems, education, English, mathematics, political science and government, science, social studies, and sociology.

The degrees awarded include: Bachelor of Arts, Bachelor of Science, Bachelor of Science in Business Administration and Bachelor of Science in Education.

FEES

Cost per academic year: tuition $3500, room and board $3000.

VIRGINIA SEMINARY AND COLLEGE

Virginia Seminary and College is a small private college founded near the end of the ninetheenth century to train youth for Christian service.

LOCATION

The ten-acre campus is located near the Blue Ridge Parkway, approximately 60 miles east of the West Virginia border and 125 miles east of Richmond, Virginia's state capital.

The Address: **Virginia Seminary and College**
2058 Garfield Avenue
Lynchburg, Virginia 24501
Telephone: (804) 528-5276

THE INSTITUTE

The focus of the college program is on Christian education and the baccalaureate degree is offered in business education, mathematics, social studies and theology.

FEES

The cost to attend the college depends upon the number of credit hours of course work selected. The cost per credit hours is $50. The maximum hours a student may carry varies between nine and twelve hours. Room and board per semester: $1,200.

DISTINGUISHED ALUMNI

Dr. Ralph Reavis -   Church Historian, Virginia University

VIRGINIA STATE UNIVERSITY

The college was established and chartered in 1882. The first instruction at the postsecondary level was offered in 1883 and the first baccalaureate degree was awarded in 1889.

CHRONOLOGY OF NAME CHANGES

1882 - Virginia Normal and Collegiate Institute
1902 - Virginia Normal and Industrial Institute
1930 - Virginia State College for Negroes
1946 - Virginia State College
1979 - Virginia State University

LOCATION

The campus is less than twenty-five miles north of Richmond, the state capital. The largest metropolitan area is Washington, D.C., approximately 135 miles north of the campus. Mass transit busy system, passenger rail service and an airport 30 miles from the campus provide adequate transportation to and from the campus.

The Address: **Virginia State University**
P.O. Box 18
Petersburg, Virginia 23803
Telephone: (804) 524-5902

THE INSTITUTION

The enrollment averages 3500 per semester on a campus area of more than 230 acres. On-campus residence halls house forty-eight percent of the student body. The student/faculty ratio is fifteen-to-one. The campus offers cooperative baccalaureate programs in engineering technology and nursing with other Virginia public colleges and universities. The baccalaureate is also offered in accounting, agriculture, animal science, biology, business administration, chemistry, communications, computer science, ecology, education, food technology, foreign language, geology, health and physical education, history, home economics, hotel and restaurant management, international studies, mathematics, music, physics, political science, psychology, public administration, social science, and sociology.

FEES

Cost per academic year: tuition $4000, room $1800, board $1500.

DISTINGUISHED ALUMNI

Reginald F. Lewis, LLB	- President/CEO TLC Beatrice Int'l Holdings, Inc.
W. Clinton Pettus	- 1991 NAFEO Distinguished Alumni
Hugh H. Smythe	- Former Ambassador to Syria
Gary Dent	- Senior Administrator, General Motors
Artrelle M. Wheatley	- Director, Academic Services University of Virgin Islands
Luther H. Foster	- 4th President, Tuskegee University

VIRGINIA UNION UNIVERSITY

Virginia Union is a private institute affiliated with the American Baptist Church. It was established in 1865 and offered the first instruction at the postsecondary level that same year. The first baccalaureate was awarded in 1899.

CHRONOLOGY OF NAME CHANGES

1865 - Wayland Academy
1899 - Virginia Union University

LOCATION

Located in Richmond, the capital city of Virginia, the campus is served by mass transit bus system, an airport less than ten miles away as well as passenger rail service just two miles away.

The Address: **Virginia Union University**
1500 North Lombardy Street
Richmond, VA 23220
Telephone: (804) 257-5881
1-800-368-3227

THE INSTITUTION

The university has an average enrollment of 1200 students and on-campus residence halls house sixty-six percent of the student body. The campus area covers 58 acres. The student/faculty ratio is fifteen-to-one. The bachelor's degree is offered in accounting, biology, business administration, chemistry, education, engineering, English history, journalism, mathematics, music, political science, psychology, public administration, religion, social welfare, sociology and theology.

<u>FEES</u>

Cost per academic year: tuition $4500, room $1500, board $2000.

<u>DISTINGUISHED ALUMNI</u>

Lawrence Douglas Wilder	-	The nation's highest ranking African-American elected state official and the first elected African-American Governor in the United States.
Adam Clayton Powell Sr.	-	Minister, Politician Civil Rights Activist
Benjamin E. Mays Ph.D	-	Preacher and Educator 1st African-American President of Atlanta's Board of Education
Spottswood W. Robinson III	-	U.S. Circuit Judge, District of Columbia Circuit
Charles Spurgeon Johnson	-	1st African-American President of Fisk University
Janet Jones	-	1986 National President AKA Sorority
Samuel L. Gravely Jr.	-	Navy's 1st African-American Admiral
Rondle E. Edwards	-	Asst. State Superintendent for Public Instruction, VA Dept. of Education

West Virginia

2 H/PBCUs

BLUEFIELD STATE COLLEGE

One of the two historically Black colleges in the state of West Virginia, Bluefield State College was established in 1895. The first instruction at the postsecondary level was offered in 1931. The first baccalaureate degree was awarded in 1932.

CHRONOLOGY OF NAME CHANGES

   1895   -   Bluefield Colored Institute
   1931   -   Bluefield State Teachers College
   1943   -   Bluefield State College

LOCATION

Bluefield is located in the southern most tip of the state of West Virginia, 270 miles from Charleston, the state capital. The campus is about 80 miles from Roanoke, Virginia, and less than 40 miles from the eastern Kentucky boarder.

The Address: **Bluefield State College**
219 Rock Street
Bluefield, West Virginia 24701
Telephone: (304) 327-4000

THE INSTITUTE

The 118-acre site provides a campus area of 40 acres as home to 2500 students. There is no on-campus housing for the state-supported co-educational institution. The college offers the associate degree as well as the bachelor's degree. Though originally one of the historically Black colleges, the population (faculty and students) is currently primarily white.

The degree programs are offered in the following areas: biological science, business and management, computer and information science, education, mathematics, physical science, social science, and interdisciplinary studies.

FEES

Cost per academic year: tuition $2500.

DISTINGUISHED ALUMNI

Obie W. O'Neal   -   Dept. Chairperson, Health & Physical Education, Albany State College

Ruth Payne Brown   -   Principal, Baltimore Unified School District

Paul Jonathan Tuffin J.D. - Magistrate, Cleveland Municipal Court, (OH)

WEST VIRGINIA STATE COLLEGE

West Virginia State, a land grant college, was charted in 1891 as a school to train Colored people. The first postsecondary level instruction was offered in 1915. The first baccalaureate degree was awarded in 1919. The college has been cited as having produced more generals than any other ROTC department at an historically Black college.

CHRONOLOGY OF NAME CHANGES

1891-	-	West Virginia Colored Institute
1915	-	West Virginia Collegiate Institute
1929	-	West Virginia State College

LOCATION

Charleston, the state capital and the nearest metropolitan city, is eight miles from campus. A mass transit bus system, an airport 15 miles from campus and passenger rail service ten miles from campus provide access to the campus.

The Address: **West Virginia State College**
Institute, West Virginia 25112
Telephone: (304) 766-3000

THE INSTITUTION

West Virginia State College is a co-educational institution with an enrollment that averages 4000 on a 93-acre area. On-campus residence halls house 12 percent of the student body. The bachelor's degree is awarded in art/advertisement, biology, building construction, business administration, chemistry communication, criminal justice, economics, education, engineering, English, history, industrial arts, mathematics, music education, political science, psychology, rehabilitation services, social welfare, and sociology. The student/faculty ratio is twenty-to-one.

FEES

Cost per academic year: tuition $3500, room and board $3200.

DISTINGUISHED ALUMNI

Joseph E. Turner	-	Brig. General
Dr. Majorie L. Harris	-	President, Lewis College of Business
Kathy Y. Mills	-	Bursar, Lincoln Univ. (PA)
Winston E. Moore	-	Penologist, Former Director of Cook County (Ill.) Department of Corrections
Dr. Morris S. Clark	-	Oral/Maxillofacial Surgeon Director, Anesthesia, University of Colorado, Health Sciences
John L. Whitehead	-	Former President, Tuskegee Airman Inc., Former Cmdr. Field Maintenance, Edwards Air Force Base, Sacramento, CA
Quentin R. Lawson	-	Executive Vice President Public Technology Inc., (D.C.)

APPENDIX A
America's 4-Year Black Colleges & Universities
An Alphabetical Listing with Local Address

Alabama A & M Univ.	P.O. Box 285	Normal	AL 35762
Alabama State Univ.	915 S. Jackson St.	Montgomery	AL 36195
Albany State College	504 College Dr.	Albany	GA 31705
Alcorn State Univ.	P.O. Box 300	Lorman	MS 39096
Allen University	1530 Harden St.	Columbia	SC 29204
Arkansas Baptist Coll.	1600 Bishop St.	Little Rock	AR 72202
Barber-Scotia College	145 Cabarrus Ave.	Concord	NC 28025
Benedict College	Harden/Blanding St.	Columbia	SC 29204
Bennett College	900 E. Washington St.	Greensboro	NC 27420
Bethune-Cookman Coll.	640 Second Ave.	Daytona Beach	FL 32015
Bloomfield College	——	Bloomfield	NJ 07003
Bluefield State College	219 Rock St.	Bluefield	WV 24701
Bowie State College	Jericho Park Rd.	Bowie	MD 20715
Central State Univ.	——	Wilberforce	OH 45384
C. Drew U. Of Medicine	120th & Wilmington	Los Angeles	CA 90059
Cheyney Univ. of Penn.	——	Cheyney	PA 19319
Chicago State Univ.	95th St. at King Dr.	Chicago	IL 60528
Claflin College	College Ave. NE	Orangeburg	SC 29115
Clark-Atlanta Univ.	240 J.P. Brawley Dr.	Atlanta	GA 30314
Coll. for Human Service	345 Hudson St.	New York	NY 10014
Coppin State College	2500 W. North Ave.	Baltimore	MD 21216
Delaware State College	1200 N.Dupoint Hwy	Dover	DE 19901
Dillard University	2601 Gentilly Blvd.	New Orleans	LA 70122
Edward Waters College	1658 Kings Rd.	Jacksonville	FL 32209
Elizabeth City State Univ.	Parkview Dr.	Elizabeth Cy	NC 27909
Fayetteville State Univ.	Murchinson Rd.	Fayetteville	NC 28301
Fisk University	1000 17th Ave.North	Nashville	TN 37203
Florida A & M Univ.	1500 Wahnish Way	Tallahassee	FL 32307
Florida Memorial College	15800 NW 42nd Ave	Miami	FL 33054
Fort Valley State College	805 State College Dr.	Fort Valley	GA 31030

Grambling State Univ.	P.O. Box 605	Grambling	LA 71245
Hampton University	West Queen St.	Hampton	VA 23668
Harris-Stowe State Coll.	3026 La Clede Ave.	St. Louis	MO 63103
Howard University	2400 Sixth St. NW	Washington	DC 20059
Huston-Tillotson College	1820 E. Eighth St.	Austin	TX 78702
Interdenominational	671 Bechwith St. SW	Atlanta	GA 30314
Jackson State Univ.	1440 J.R. Lynch St.	Jackson	MS 39217
Jarvis Christian College	HY 80 W. Drawer G	Hawkins	TX 75765
Johnson C. Smith Univ.	100-300 Bettiesford Rd.	Charlotte	NC 28216
Kentucky State Univ.	E. Main St.	Frankfort	KY 40601
Knoxville College	901 College St. W	Knoxville	TN 37921
Lane College	545 Lane Ave.	Jackson	TN 38301
Langston University	P.O. Box 907	Langston	OK 73050
LeMoyne-Owen College	807 Walker Ave.	Memphis	TN 38126
Lincoln Univ. (MO)	820 Chestnut St.	Jefferson City	MO 65101
Lincoln Univ. (PA)	Old Route 1	Lincoln Univ.	PA 19532
Livingstone College	701 W. Monroe St.	Salisbury	NC 28144
Martin University	2171 Avondate Pl.	Indianapolis	IN 46305
Marygrove College	8425 W. McNichols Rd.	Detroit	MI 48221
Medgar Evers College	1150 Carroll St.	Brooklyn	NY 11200
Meharry Medical College	1005 D B.Todd Blvd.	Nashville	TN 37208
Miles College	5500 Avenue G	Birmingham	AL 35208
Mississippi Valley St. U.	——	Itta Bena	MS 38941
Morehouse College	830 Western Dr. SW	Atlanta	GA 30314
Morehouse Med. School	720 Westview Dr. SW	Atlanta	GA 30310
Morgan State Univ.	Cold Spring Lane	Baltimore	MD 21239
Morris Brown	643 M.L. King Dr. SW	Atlanta	GA 30314
Morris College	North Main St.	Sumter	SC 29150
Norfolk State Univ.	2401 Corprew Ave.	Norfolk	VA 23504
North Carolina A & T	1601 E. Market St.	Greensboro	NC 27411
North Carolina Central	1801 Fayetteville St.	Durham	NC 27707
Oakwood College	Oakwood Road	Huntsville	AL 35806
Paine College	1235 15th St.	Augusta	GA 30910
Paul Quinn College	3837 Simpson Stuart Rd	Dallas	TX 75241
Philander Smith College	812 W. 13th St.	Little Rock	AR 72203

Prairie View A & M Univ.	P.O. Box 66	Prairie View	TX 77445
Rust College	——	Holly Springs	MI 38635
St. Augustine's College	——	Raleigh	NC 27611
Saint Paul's College	406 Windsor Ave.	Lawrenceville	VA 23868
Savannah State College	P.O. Box 20449	Savannah	GA 31404
Selma University	——	Selma	AL 36701
Shaw University	118 E. South St.	Raleigh	NC 27602
Simmons U.. Bible Coll.	1811 Dumesnil St.	Louisville	KY 40210
Sojourner-Douglass	500 N. Caroline St.	Baltimore	MD 21205
South Carolina State	P.O. Box 1568	Orangeburg	SC 29117
Southern Univ.-B.R.	P.O. Box 9614	Baton Rouge	LA 70813
Southern Univ.-Law Sch.	P.O. Box 9614	Baton Rouge	LA 70813
Southern Univ.-N.O.	6400 Press Dr.	New Orleans	LA 70126
Southern Univ.-Shrev.	——	Shreveport	LA 71107
Spelman College	350 Spelman Lane	Atlanta	GA 30314
Stillman College	P.O. Box Drawer 1430	Tuscaloosa	AL 35403
Talladega College	627 W. Battle St.	Talladega	AL 35160
Tennessee State Univ.	3500 Centennial Blvd.	Nashville	TN 37203
Texas College	2404 N. Grand Ave.	Tyler	TX 75702
Texas Southern Univ.	3100 Cleburne Ave.	Houston	TX 77004
Tougaloo College	——	Tougaloo	MI 39174
Tuskegee University	——	Tuskegee	AL 36088
Univ. of Arkansas-PB	N. Cedar St.	Pine Bluff	AK 71601
Univ. of Dist. Columbia	4200 Conneticut Ave.	Washington	DC 20008
Univ. of Maryland-E.S.	——	Princess Anne	MD 21853
Univ. of Virgin Islands	St. Thomas	U.S. Virgin Islands	00802
Virginia Seminary	2058 Garfield Ave.	Lynchburg	VA 24501
Virginia State Univ.	——	Petersburg	VA 23803
Virginia Union Univ.	1500 N. Lombardy St.	Richmond	VA 23220
Voorhees College	——	Denmark	SC 29042
West VA State	——	Institute	WV 25112
Wilberforce Univ.	——	Wilberforce	OH 45384
Wiley College	71 Rosborough Sp. Rd.	Marshall	TX 75670
Winston-Salem State U.	601 MLK Jr. Dr.	Winston Salem	NC 27110
Xavier University	7325 Palmentto/Pine	New Orleans	LA 70125

APPENDIX B
America's 4-Year Black Colleges & Universities
By State & Athletic Association Affiliation

ALABAMA
Alabama Agricultural and Mechanical University[2]
Alabama State University[1]
Miles College
Oakwood College
Selma University
Stillman College[3]
Talladega College[4]
Tuskegee University[2]

ARKANSAS
Arkansas Baptist College[4]
Philander Smith College
University of Arkansas at Pine Bluff[4]

CALIFORNIA
Charles R. Drew University of Medicine and Science

DELAWARE
Delaware State College

DISTRICT OF COLUMBIA
Howard University[1]
University of the District of Columbia[2]

FLORIDA
Bethune-Cookman College
Edward Waters College[4]
Florida Agricultural and Mechanical University[1]
Florida Memorial College

GEORGIA
Albany State College[2]
Clark Atlanta University[2]

Superscripts 1, 2, 3:   National Collegiate Athletic Association
                        Divisions 1, 2 and 3
        Superscript 4: National Association Intercollegiate Athletics

GEORGIA cont.
 Fort Valley State College[2]
 Interdenominational Theological Center
 Morehouse College[2]
 Morehouse School of Medicine
 Morris Brown College[2]
 Paine College
 Savannah State College
 Spelman College

ILLINOIS
 Chicago State University[1,4]

INDIANA
 Martin University

KENTUCKY
 Kentucky State University[2,4]
 Simmons Bible College

LOUISIANA
 Dillard University[4]
 Grambling State University[1]
 Southern University - Baton Rouge
 Southern University - New Orleans[3,4]
 Southern University - Shreveport
 Southern University Law Center (SULA)
 Xavier University[4]

MARYLAND
 Bowie State College[2,4]
 Coppin State College
 Morgan State University[2]
 Sojourner-Douglass College
 University of Maryland - Eastern Shore[1]

MICHIGAN
 Marygrove College

Superscripts 1, 2, 3: National Collegiate Athletic Association
                       Divisions 1, 2 and 3
    Superscript 4: National Association Intercollegiate Athletics

MISSISSIPPI
Alcorn State University[1]
Jackson State University
Mississippi Valley State University[1,4]
Rust College[3]
Tougaloo College[3]

MISSOURI
Harris-Stowe State College
Lincoln University[2]

NEW JERSEY
Bloomfield College

NEW YORK
College for Human Services
Medgar Evers College (CUNY)[3]

NORTH CAROLINA
Barber-Scotia College[4]
Bennett College
Elizabeth City State University[2]
Fayetteville State University[2]
Johnson C. Smith University[2]
Livingstone College[2]
North Carolina Agricultural and Technical State University[1]
North Carolina Central University[2]
Saint Augustine's College[2]
Shaw University
Winston-Salem State University[2]

OHIO
Central State University[2]
Wilberforce University

OKLAHOMA
Langston University[4]

PENNSYLVANIA
Cheyney University[1,2]
Lincoln University[4]

Superscripts 1, 2, 3: **National Collegiate Athletic Association Divisions 1, 2 and 3**
Superscript 4: **National Association Intercollegiate Athletics**

SOUTH CAROLINA
Allen University
Benedict College[2]
Claflin College
Morris Colege[4]
South Carolina State College[1]
Voorhees College[4]

TENNESSEE
Fisk University[3]
Knoxville College[3]
Lane College[3]
LeMoyne-Owen College[3,4]
Meharry Medical College
Tennessee State University[1]

TEXAS
Huston-Tillotson College
Jarvis Christian College
Paul Quinn College
Prairie View A & M University[1,4]
Texas College[4]
Texas Southern University[1]
Wiley College

U.S. VIRGIN ISLANDS
University of the Virgin Islands - St. Thomas & St. Croix

VIRGINIA
Hampton University[2,4]
Norfolk State University[2]
Saint Paul's College[2]
Virginia Seminary and College
Virginia State University[2]
Virginia Union University[2]

WEST VIRGINIA
Bluefield State College[4]
West Virginia State College[4]

Superscripts 1, 2, 3: National Collegiate Athletic Association
Divisions 1, 2 and 3
Superscript 4: National Association Intercollegiate Athletics

APPENDIX C
Black Colleges & Universities Supported by the United Negro College Fund

Barber-Scotia College

Benedict College

Bennett College

Bethune-Cookman College

Claflin College

Clark-Atlanta University

Dillard University

Edward Waters College

Fisk University

Florida Memorial College

Huston-Tillotson College

Interdenominational Theological Ctr.

Jarvis Christian College

Johnson C. Smith Unversity

Knoxville College

Lane College

LeMoyne-Owen College

Livingstone College

Miles College

Morehouse College

Morris College

Morris Brown College

Oakwood College

Paine College

Paul Quinn College

Philander Smith College

Rust College

Saint Augustine's College

Saint Paul's College

Shaw University

Spelman College

Stillman College

Talladega College

Texas College

Tougaloo College

Tuskegee University

Virginia Union University

Wilberforce University

Wiley College

Xavier University

Voorhees College

APPENDIX D
Church-Related Black Colleges & Universities

AFRICAN METHODIST EPISCOPAL
    Allen University   (OH)
    Edward Waters College   (FL)
    Morris Brown College   (GA)
    Paul Quinn College   (TX)
    Wilberforce University   (OH)

AFRICAN METHODIST EPISCOPAL ZION
    Livingstone College   (NC)

BAPTIST
    Arkansas Baptist College   (AK)
    Benedict College   (SC)
    Florida Memorial College   (FL)
    Morris College   (SC)
    Selma University   (AL)
    Shaw University   (NC)
    Spelman College   (GA)
    Virginia Union University   (VA)

CHRISTIAN CHURCH (DISCIPLES OF CHRIST)
    Jarvis Christian College   (TX)

CHRISTIAN METHODIST EPISCOPAL
    Lane College   (TN)
    Miles College   (AL)
    Texas College   (TX)

INTERDENOMINATIONAL
    Interdenominational Theological Center (GA)

MULTIPLE PROTESTANT DENOMINATIONS
    Dillard University   (LA)
    Huston-Tillotson College   (TX)
    LeMoyne-Owen College   (TN)
    Paine College   (GA)

PRESBYTERIAN, U.S.

Bloomfield College	(NJ)
Stillman College	(AL)

PROTESTANT EPISCOPAL

Saint Augustine's College	(NC)
Saint Paul's College	(VA)
Voorhees College	(SC)

ROMAN CATHOLIC

Marygrove College	(MI)
Xavier University Of Louisiana	(LA)

SEVENTH DAY ADVENTIST

Oakwood College	(AL)

UNITED CHURCH OF CHRIST

Fisk University	(TN)
Talladega College	(AL)
Tougaloo College	(MS)

UNITED METHODIST

Bennett College	(NC)
Bethune-Cookman College	(FL)
Claflin College	(SC)
Clark/Atlanta University	(GA)
Philander Smith College	(AR)
Rust College	(MS)
Wiley College	(TX)

UNITED PRESBYTERIAN, U.S.A.

Johnson C. Smith University	(NC)
Knoxville College	(TN)
Barber-Scotia College	(NC)

APPENDIX E
Black Colleges & Universities
Conferring Doctorates

Charles R. Drew University of Medicine and Science

Clark Atlanta University

Florida Agricultural and Mechanical University

Howard University

Interdenominational Theological Center

Jackson State University

Meharry Medical College

Morehouse Medical College

Morgan State University

South Carolina State College

Southern University (BR)

Tennessee State University

Texas Southern University

University of Maryland - Eastern Shore

APPENDIX F
"Firsts" In African-American History

First public schools for Negroes and Indians – Virginia 1620

First Negro college graduate from an American College – John Russworm, 1826, Bowdoin, Maine

First school for African-Americans in Cincinnati – paid for by African-Americans – 1834

First African-American to receive a degree from a theological seminary in the United States – Theodore S. Wright (Princeton, 1836)

First African-American graduate from West Point – Henry O. Flipper – 1877

First woman to preside over the U.S. Senate – Blanche K. Bruce – 1879

First training school for African-American nurses – Providence Hospital – 1889

First African-American to receive the Ph.D. from Harvard – W.E.B. DuBois – 1895

First African-American woman to head a major public university on the west coast – Jewel Plummer Cobb – Former President CSU, Fullerton

First African-American Rhodes Scholar – Alain Leroy Locke – a Howard University graduate

First African-American woman appointed to the board of education in Washington, D.C. – Mary Church Terrell

First African-American to serve as President of a Catholic institution – Patrick Francis Healy – Georgetown University, 1874

Only training site for African-American pilots , the Tuskegee Airmen, during World War II – Tuskegee University.

Bibliography

Barrons's Profiles of American Colleges. 7th Edition. Barron's Educational Series Inc. New York, 1991.

Christa Brelin, Editor. *Who's Who Among Black Americans. 7th Edition.* Gale Research Inc. Detroit, MI. 1991.

Susan W. Dilts. *Peterson's Four-Year Colleges.* Princeton, New Jersey, 1991.

Edward B. Fiske. *The Fiske Guide To Colleges, 1991.* Random House Inc. New York, 1990.

Romeo Garrett. *Famous First Facts About Negroes.* 1972.

Institutional and Presidential Profiles. NAFEO. Black Higher Education Center. Washington, D.C. 1988.

H. A. Ploski and James Williams. *The Negro Almanac.* Gale Research Inc. Detroit, MI. 1989.

M. R. Rodenhouse, Editor. *The HEP-1992 Higher Education Directory.* Higher Education Publication, Inc. Fall Church, VA.

Darren L. Smith, Editor. *Black Americans Information Directory.* Gale Research Inc. Detroit, MI. 1991.

Charles T. Straughn II and B. Lovejoy Straughn. *Lovejoy's College Guide. 50th Edition.* Prentice Hall, N.Y. 1991.

The College Blue Book, Macmillian Publishing Co. New York, 1989.

Index

Index

For your notes:

For your notes:

For your notes:

For your notes: